Thames Essay No. 49

Economic Impact of Generalized Tariff Preferences

BY

Rolf J. Langhammer

and

André Sapir

Gower

Aldershot · Brookfield USA · Hong Kong · Singapore · Sydney

for the
TRADE POLICY RESEARCH CENTRE
London

First published 1987 by

Gower Publishing Company Limited
Gower House, Croft Road, Aldershot, Hampshire GU11 3HR
United Kingdom

Gower Publishing Company
Old Post Road, Brookfield, Vermont 05036
United States of America

Gower Publishing Australia
85 Whiting Street, Artamon, New South Wales 2064,
Australia

ISSN 0306-6991
ISBN 0566 05338 1

British Library Cataloguing-in-Publication Data
Langhammer, Rolf J.
    Economic Impact of Generalized Tariff Preferences.
    1. Tariff Preferences
    I. Title II. Sapir, André.
    382.7'3   HF1721

Library of Congress Cataloging-in-Publication Data
Langhammer, Rolf. J.
    Economic Impact of Generalized Tariff Preferences.
    (Thames Essay No. 49]
    Bibliography: p.82
    1. Tariff Preferences.
    2. Tariff Preferences—United States.
    3. Tariff Preferences—European Economic Community
Countries. 4. Developing Countries—Commerce.
    I. Sapir, André. II. Title. III. Series:
HF1721.L35   1987   382.7'53   87-15045

Printed in the United Kingdom by
Biddles Ltd, Guildford, Surrey

Contents

LIST OF TABLES   vii

BIOGRAPHICAL NOTES   viii

PREFACE   x

1   RATIONALE OF THE GENERALIZED SYSTEM
OF PREFERENCES   1
Birth of the GATT   1
Developing Countries in the GATT   3
UNCTAD and the Debate over Preferences   7
GSP within the GATT   11
Outline of the Study   12

2   NATURE AND COVERAGE OF TWO GSP SCHEMES   16
GSP Scheme of the United States   16
   Product Coverage   18
   Limitations on Preferential Treatment   18
GSP Scheme of the European Community   19
   Country Coverage   20
   Product Coverage   21
   Limitations on Preferential Treatment   21
Comparison of the Schemes   25

3 TRADE EFFECTS OF THE MAIN GSP SCHEMES 29
Theory and Measurement 29
Trade Effects of the American Scheme 32
Trade Effects of the Community Scheme 35
Comparison of the Trade Effects 39
Export-oriented Investments and GSP
    Restrictions 41

4 DISTRIBUTION OF BENEFITS FROM GSP SCHEMES 48
The American Scheme 49
The European Community Scheme 52
Distribution of Benefits Compared 57

5 ADMINISTRATIVE RULES AND THEIR TRADE
    EFFECTS 60
Rules and Limitations of the American Scheme 60
European Community Scheme Rules 63
Comparison of Administrative Rules 66
Trade Effects of the GSP 67

6 REVIEW OF THE GSP AND ITS FUTURE PROSPECTS 69
Objectives of the GSP 71
GSP in the 1970s 72
Is the GSP Worthy of Reform? 74
What is at Stake? 75
    Principle of Graduation 75
    Reduction of Tariffs 78
The Future of the GSP 79

List of References 82

List of Thames Essays 86

List of Tables

3.1   US Imports: Total, MFN-Dutiable, and
GSP Coverage   40

3.2   Percentage Share of GSP-receiving Imports
in GSP-covered Imports of the European
Community, 1978-83   42

4.1   US Imports, Duties and Preference
Margins for Beneficiary Countries with
over $100 million of GSP-eligible Imports,
1979   50

4.2   Community Imports of GSP Products from
the Ten Largest Beneficiaries, 1973 and
1983   54

5.1   Utilization Rate of Tariff Quotas for
Sensitive GSP Items on the West German
Market 1977 and 1982, by Major
Beneficiaries   65

Biographical Notes

ROLF J. LANGHAMMER is a Senior Research Fellow at the Institut für Weltwirtschaft, Kiel, in the Federal Republic of Germany. He was previously a Research Associate in the Department of Economics, Kiel University (1972-77), where he obtained his doctorate. Dr Langhammer has mainly written on patterns of international trade, trade policy and economic integration. He has been a consultant to various government departments in the Federal Republic of Germany, to the Commission of the European Community in Brussels (1984-85) and to the International Labour Office in Geneva (1985). He is the co-author of *The Second Englargement of the European Community: Adjustment Requirements and the Challenge for Policy Reform* (1982) and the principal author of *EC Trade Policies towards Associated Developing Countries: Barriers to Success* (1985).

ANDRÉ SAPIR has been Professor of Economics at the Free University of Brussels, in Belgium, since 1981 and a Research Fellow at the Centre for European Policy Studies, also in Brussels, since 1983. He graduated from the Free University of Brussels in 1972 and obtained his doctorate at Johns Hopkins University, Baltimore, in the United States of America in 1977. He subsequently taught at the University of Wisconsin; and in 1986-87 he was a Visiting Professor of Economics at the Institut Universitaire de Hautes Etudes

Internationales, University of Geneva. Professor Sapir has been a consultant to the World Bank of Washington, to the Organisation for Economic Cooperation and Development in Paris and to the Secretariat of the United Nations Conference on Trade and Development in Geneva. He is co-author of *Trade in Services: Economic Determinants and Development-related Issues* (1981) and has had a number of articles published in professional journals.

Preface

RELATIONS between developed and developing countries in the international trading system, whose norms, rules and procedures are set out in the General Agreement on Tariffs and Trade (GATT), have been reaching an *impasse*. For a quarter of a century, the developed countries have been allowing, or encouraging, the developing countries to become contracting parties to the GATT without requiring them to abide by the more important obligations of membership. What is more, they have acquiesced in the formal derogation from the principle of non-discrimination, which is the keystone of the GATT, to permit the Generalized System of Preferences (GSP) in favour of developing countries to be established and maintained.

At the same time, developing countries — especially the more advanced ones — have been faced with discriminatory protection against them whenever their exports have been uncomfortably successful in the markets of developed countries, such protection often taking the form of export-restraint arrangements negotiated 'outside' the framework of GATT norms, rules and procedures.

The costs to developing countries of limitations on their access to the markets of developed countries are not so much offset as multiplied by their more or less complete freedom to establish and maintain trade regimes which are highly protectionist and Byzantine in their complexity.

By the early 1980s, it was clear that the role of developing countries in the international trading system was bound to attract increasing attention, especially if a new 'round' of multilateral trade negotiations under GATT auspices was to be undertaken. Accordingly, the Trade Policy Research Centre, with the help of a grant from the Leverhulme Trust in London, embarked in 1983 on a major programme of studies on the Participation of Developing Countries in the International Trading System, supervised by Martin Wolf, the Centre's Director of Studies.

The purpose of the programme has been to clarify, for public discussion and policy formation, the underlying reasons for the current difficulties in relations between developed and developing countries in the GATT system. The programme focusses both on economic and legal issues in the GATT system *per se* and on impediments to trade liberalization in individual developing countries. The emphasis on the latter derived from the perception that the GATT framework of norms, rules and procedures can be no more than the 'handmaiden' of trade liberalization. Liberalization will not be brought about, however, unless there is a consensus in the countries concerned on both its feasibility and its value in promoting their economic growth and development. The domestic impediments to trade liberalization have to be understood if they are to be overcome.

It is true for all countries that multilateral negotiations are a means more of achieving the trade liberalization that is already widely understood to be in each country's own interests than of liberalizing when no such benefit is seen. In other words, reciprocal bargaining is a way of overcoming domestic resistance to the trade liberalization that is strongly desired by prevailing forces in each country, both in government and in society at large. A desire to liberalize, almost irrespective of what happens elsewhere, is particularly significant in small countries. The smaller the country, the less effective is its international bargaining power and, therefore, the less persuasive is the argument that improved access to markets abroad depends on the liberalization of access to its own market. For this reason, smaller countries usually liberalize only if there is a strong domestic consensus that such liberalization is in their own interests, such a consensus having been long established in countries like Sweden, Switzerland and Singapore.

In developing the programme of studies it was clear that both the trade policies of developing countries and the role of those countries in the international trading system reflect economic ideas that have found legal expression in the GATT and associated codes. In particular, developing countries have consistently denied the relevance to themselves of the twin GATT concepts of 'equal treatment' and reciprocal trade liberalization. Arguing that 'equal treatment of unequals is unfair', developing countries have demanded discrimination in their favour under the general rubric of 'special and differential treatment' or, more recently, 'differential and more favourable treatment'. Arguing that reliance on the market thwarts economic development, developing countries have insisted on their need to introduce protection at home while receiving market access and preferential treatment abroad.

Drafts of the papers arising from the Centre's programme of studies were presented at a three-day research meeting at Wiston House, near Steyning, in the United Kingdom, in October 1984, attended by those engaged on the programme and a number of other scholars and officials. The meeting was immediately preceded by a two-day meeting, also at Wiston House, of a study group which is drawing together the conclusions of the programme of studies. This meeting, too, was attended by a number of officials. The two international meetings were funded by a grant from the Ford Foundation in New York, while the programme of studies as a whole has been founded by the Levehulme Trust in London.

The authors are grateful to Tracy Murray and Martin Wolf for critical comments which have greatly improved the quality of the Essay. They would also like to thank A. Belkora and other participants of a research meeting held at the Wiston House for helpful comments. Special thanks are due to Margot Müller of the Institut für Weltwirtschaft in Kiel for carefully preparing the typescript.

As usual, it has to be stressed that the views expressed in this Thames Essay do not necessarily represent those of members of the Council or those of the staff and associates of the Trade Policy Research Centre which, having general terms of reference, does not represent a consensus of opinion on any particular issue. The purpose of the Centre is to promote independent analysis and public discussion of international economic policy issues.

HUGH CORBET
Director
Trade Policy Research Centre

London
May 1987

Chapter 1

Rationale of the Generalized System of Preferences

WITH THE guns of World War II still firing, a number of foreign policy leaders and economists from the United States and the United Kingdom began to envisage the establishment, at the conclusion of hostilities, of a new world trading system[1]. Mindful of the experience of the late 1920s and 1930s when protectionist and discriminatory practices had got out of hand they favoured a liberal, and in the case of the Americans at least, a non-discriminatory system, within which world trade could be expected to expand.[2] Along with the growth of trade, world income would rise and world peace would be secured.

Birth of the GATT

Immediately after the war, negotiations were undertaken to agree on an institutional framework for the new trading regime. In order to translate their vision into reality, however, the US Administration needed domestic as well as foreign support. Despite a general mood in favour of a more liberal international trading order, there was still considerable domestic opposition to trade liberalization at home. Under pressure from Congress, the Administration had to recognise that protection to particular industries would have to be permitted in certain circumstances. As one commentator has noted, 'these developments indicate that the United States trade policy commitment at the beginning of the post-war period was to a policy of liberal trade rather than to a policy of free trade'.[3]

Unlike the United States, most of her trading partners emerged from World War II with a greatly impaired economic base and their support for liberal trade policies was correspondingly weaker. Many were determined to continue to use their existing trade restrictions in the form either of conventional protectionism or of preferences for some trading partners and discrimination against others.

The initial American proposals for an International Trade Organization (ITO) were amended during negotiations with main trading partners and a final document, aimed at establishing the ITO and known as the Havana Charter, was drawn up in 1948. Meanwhile, the General Agreement on Tariffs and Trade (GATT), based on the commercial policy provisions in the Havana Charter, had been agreed in 1947 in order to provide a framework for tariff negotiations. After the failure of the United States Congress to ratify the Havana Charter, the GATT assumed the commercial policy role designed for the stillborn ITO. Nearly 40 years later, the GATT, which even now is governed only by a protocol of provisional application, still constitutes the only available legal framework for much of world trade.

The GATT is based on the principle of non-discrimination, enshrined in its first article, which requires that each nation extend equal treatment to all its partners (Contracting Parties of the GATT) in merchandise trade. This rule is known as the Most-Favoured-Nation (MFN) clause. A major exception to this rule was permitted, however, in that existing preferential tariff arrangements were allowed to continue. The exception was granted after the United Kingdom refused to agree to the abolition of the preferential tariff system established among Commonwealth countries in 1932.[4] This departure from the MFN principle was to have long-lasting consequences.

Reciprocity is the fundamental technique of trade bargaining in the GATT. In order to reduce trade barriers and thereby improve the treatment of trade partners, the GATT established a procedure for bargaining that operated through seven successive rounds of multilateral trade negotiations from 1947 to 1979. Central to this procedure is the requirement of reciprocity which reflects the political reality of the mercantilist pressures that make unilateral liberalization extraordinarily difficult. The principle of reciprocity was of particular importance in the United States where it was seen as an appropriate way of using the carrot of access to the huge American market to bring about global liberalization.

DEVELOPING COUNTRIES IN THE GATT

One of the major problems in the construction and operation of the international trading system after World War II has concerned relations between the developed and the developing countries. In the original American proposals for an ITO, it was argued that the developing countries 'could best develop by participating fully in a multilateral non-discriminatory system with the lowest possible levels of tariffs and no quantitative restrictions'.[5] This position was rejected by the developing countries in the ITO negotiations. Instead, they insisted on commitments by the international community (a) to further their level of development and (b) to be excepted from many of the rules on commercial policy. In the end, the Havana Charter contained a number of provisions especially favouring developing countries but, owing to the failure of the ITO, most of these provisions were abandoned, with the exception of certain commercial policy measures that were incorporated in the GATT. In particular, Article XVIII of the General Agreement grants developing countries additional flexibility in their trade regimes (i) to foster particular infant industries and (ii) to apply quantitative restrictions in case of balance of payments difficulties.

Developing countries played only a minor role in the birth of the GATT and their participation in the early rounds of multilateral trade negotiations remained minimal. Apart from the fact that many developing countries were not politically independent at the time, their lack of participation was mostly the consequence of the combination of non-discrimination and reciprocity especially as the latter applied in the early GATT negotiating process.[6] In the first place, under the 'dominant supplier' rule in operation at the time, the major tariff negotiations were concentrated on manufactured goods traded primarily among the developed countries, while the concessions made were applied to all GATT members on the MFN principle.[7] In the second place, the inward-looking trade strategies adopted by the developing countries made them unwilling to bargain on the basis of reciprocity by offering reductions in their own tariffs.

A turning point in the GATT's relations with the developing countries occurred in 1958 with the publication of the Haberler Report on trends in international trade.[8] The report argued that the exports of developing countries were lagging behind the growth of world trade generally and it imputed an important part of responsibility for this to the trade policies of the developed countries. The GATT responded by establishing a committee to investigate the extent to which the developed countries were impeding the exports of the developing countries. The committee arrived at the following conclusions:

(i) only few of the tariff concessions made in the GATT rounds up to then had been on items considered at the time to be of export interest to the developing countries;[9]

(ii) tariffs on manufactured products of interest to the developing countries were generally higher than duties on items exported by the developed countries;

(iii) tariffs in developed countries discriminated among the developing countries on the basis of origin as a result of such arrangements as Commonwealth preferences or the preferences granted by the newly-created European Economic Community to its African associates;

(iv) the tariff structure in the developed countries discriminated against the development of processing industries in the developing countries;

(v) quantitative restrictions were at least as damaging as tariffs in terms of both their levels and their structure; and

(vi) various other measures in the developed countries (such as internal taxes) also discriminated against exports of the developing countries.

In the meantime, the developing countries had begun to press harder for changes in the international trading system in order to expand their non-traditional exports and thereby foster their industrialization and development. One reason for the increased pressure was the newly-acquired independence of many developing countries; another was the urge towards economic development that was shared by all the poor nations. Yet another reason was the gradual change in attitude towards inward-looking trade strategies, as the difficulties of developing countries, whose development was based on import-substitution policies, especially the countries in Latin America, became more evident. By the early 1960s the pressure for changes in the rules governing the policies affecting trade between the developed and the developing countries had grown very strong. One opportunity for progress was the GATT-sponsored Kennedy Round of multilateral trade negotiations for which preparatory work was under way. Accordingly, during the GATT ministerial meeting held in 1963, a number of interesting initiatives were launched.

First, the Contracting Parties to GATT endorsed, with reservations, the action programme initiated by a group of developing countries. The programme was a consequence of the Haberler Report and it called, among other things, for a commitment by the developed countries to eliminate all trade barriers facing exports from the developing countries.

The developed countries were sharply divided in their attitude toward the action programme. The main division was between the United States and the European Community, a division that reflected the conflict between the insistence on non-discrimination of the former and the willingness to accept discrimination of the latter, as exemplified by the preferences granted by the Community to its African associates. The United States had more than an abstract interest in defending GATT rules in the matter of preferences. Since the Community preferences were reciprocal, the associates had to grant privileged treatment to imports from the European Community as against imports from the United States and thus, they discriminated against imports from the latter.

The second initiative at the GATT ministerial meeting of 1963 was a consequence of the Community's favourable attitude toward positive measures for increasing the export earnings of the developing countries. The Belgian representative at the ministerial meeting introduced the so-called Brasseur Plan for preferences in favour of developing countries. Under this plan, the developed countries would have granted selective, temporary and degressive preferences to the developing countries. The selective approach was designed to preserve the value of the preferences already enjoyed by the African countries associated with the European Community.

The third initiative was the modification of the legal and institutional framework of GATT to facilitate the trade of the developing countries. Two years later this initiative resulted in the addition of Part IV of the General Agreement, a largely symbolic gesture by the developed countries since the obligations contained in it were not binding. One of the main consequences of Part IV was acceptance that the developed countries would not expect reciprocity in return for commitments to reduce barriers against the exports of the developing countries.

Little of substance resulted directly from these three initiatives. The action programme was never formally adopted, the Brasseur Plan was rejected, and Part IV was mostly rhetoric. For the developing countries, the disappointment was great. While the principle of non-reciprocity had been accepted, the concessions granted by the developed countries fell short of their demands. In particular, the developing countries contested the fundamental GATT principle of MFN treatment. They argued that equal treatment of unequal partners could not constitute an equitable arrangement. These countries therefore asked for special and preferential treatment in their favour which the developed countries continued to deny them.

UNCTAD AND THE DEBATE OVER PREFERENCES

The failure of the GATT to respond to their demands prompted the developing countries to seek an alternative forum for confronting the developed countries. The narrow debate on trade and commercial policy inside the GATT was soon to be transformed into a comprehensive political debate on the whole range of economic relations between developed and developing countries. In 1962, at the initiative of the communist and the developing countries, the General Assembly of the United Nations resolved to convene an international conference on trade and development problems. After a great deal of preparatory work, the first United Nations Conference on Trade and Development (UNCTAD) met in Geneva during the spring of 1964.

The preparations for the Conference had been organised by Raúl Prebisch, an Argentinian economist who became the first Secretary-General of UNCTAD.[10] The Prebisch Report is an important document not only because it provided the major impetus for the proceedings of the first UNCTAD, but also because it still constitutes the frame of reference for the positions articulated by the developing countries. It outlined the main issues to be discussed at the Conference and proposed a comprehensive programme for dealing with them.

The report addressed the need for the developing countries to increase their exports, the slow growth of which was perceived to be the result of a persistent tendency towards external imbalance inherent in the development process. It dealt with two major problems: (i) the slow growth of earnings from exports of primary products and (ii) the need for the developing countries to export manufactured products. The solutions recommended by the Report were centred around the 'need for a positive new trade policy for development, as contrasted with the Havana Charter and GATT's allegedly negative policy of removing restrictions to trade'.[11] In the area of primary products, the Report recommended a two-pronged approach: international commodity agreements and compensatory finance. As regards manufactured products, it recommended that developed countries should grant temporary preferences to the exports of developing countries.[12]

A devaluation of the currencies of developing countries, which is a possible alternative to preferences, was rejected by the developing countries because of the negative effect it would have on their export earnings from traditional commodity exports. Preferences, however, were looked upon as a way of improving the competitive position of developing country exporters *vis à vis* competing producers in non-beneficiary exporting countries as well as home producers in the so-called donor countries. The recommendation for preferences envisaged free entry for exports of manufactures of the developing countries into the markets of the developed countries for a ten-year period for each product from the time a country started to export it. Developing countries would thus be granted temporary protection against competition from rivals in the richer countries.

It is important to underscore the fact that the preferential tariff system offered two conceptually distinct avenues for achieving its objective of expanding manufactured exports from developing countries: (i) the elimination of tariffs and (ii) preferential treatment over competitors from the developed countries. The arguments put forward by the proponents of preferences emphasised the latter aspect. In the Prebisch Report, the economic rationale for preferences was developed in terms of the infant-industry and economies of scale arguments. The infant-industry argument postulates a divergence of social from private returns in the manufacturing sector of developing countries resulting in under-investment; the economies of scale argument assumes that domestic markets in developing countries are too small to establish industry on a cost-effective scale. In both cases, it was argued that preferences would provide the necessary incentive for investment in industry in developing countries through opportunity for higher profits. Although discriminatory treatment was clearly the priority for the supporters of preferences, they also recognised the importance of the reduction of MFN tariffs *per se*, especially if high tariffs were to be cut disproportionately (through formulas for tariff harmonization). The desire to reduce the disparities in tariffs was motivated by the tariff structure of the developed countries which had been shown to discriminate against the processing of raw materials by the developing countries.

The opponents of preferences rejected the reasoning in favour of preferential treatment by alleging a lack of theoretical and empirical evidence in support of the infant-industry and economies of scale arguments. They were, however, divided in their attitude toward tariff reduction. Those who favoured it emphasized that the tariff structures in developed countries were indeed a strong deterrent to industrialization in the developing countries. Those opposed to tariff reductions suggested that the major reason for the lack of success by developing countries in exporting manufactured products lay rather in their own import-substitution policies and subsequent currency over-valuation. They favoured a policy reform in developing countries encompassing the removal of factor and goods price distortions and including currency devaluations.

The issue of tariff preferences produced an intense debate among the 120 participating countries at the first UNCTAD meeting in 1964. The developing countries gave nearly unanimous support to preferences and, despite wide differences among them on the precise nature of such preferences, they succeeded in agreeing on a joint recommendation. The situation was quite different among the developed countries who showed sharp divisions, especially between the West European countries and the United States. In Western Europe, the idea of preferences was generally accepted, but there were differences of view on existing preferential agreements. The British favoured across-the-board preferences for all developing countries, while the European Community favoured a selective approach that would safeguard preferences enjoyed by its African associates. The United States, however, rejected the principle of preferences outright. The American attitude eventually forced the developing countries to withdraw their joint recommendation.

The American opposition to preferences at UNCTAD was upheld by domestic supporters both of protection and of free trade. The former group was against any tariff concessions because of its fear of additional imports. The position of the free-traders was based on their determination to uphold the principle of non-discriminatory treatment in trade.

After the experience of UNCTAD, the United States found itself 'politically virtually isolated from all the developing countries and most of the developed countries as well'.[13] The country was therefore faced with the need to reconsider its policy towards the developing countries. Essentially, the United States had two main options in drafting a policy to deal with the trade problems of these nations. The first one consisted of a move towards free trade, either unilateral or multilateral, in products of interest to the developing countries. The other was to accept the idea of preferences. Despite a general commitment within the United States to a liberal trading system, political reality forced the American Administration to adopt the second option. In particular, there was considerable fear of a trend towards the regionalization of world trade under the impetus of the European Community and of subsequent discrimination against American exports in the markets of developing countries. Accordingly, in 1967, the United States announced its acceptance of the principle of non-discriminatory preferences for all developing countries.

The shift of position by the United States paved the way for the formal acceptance by the developed countries of the principle of preferential tariff treatment in favour of developing nations. This principle was formally accepted at the second session of UNCTAD held in 1968. Under the unanimously agreed Generalized System of Preferences (GSP), developing countries would be charged no duty for their exports to the developed countries, while each developed country would continue to levy the MFN tariff on products from other developed countries. The GSP would thus provide the developing countries with a margin of preference equal to the MFN tariff in the developed nations.

GSP WITHIN THE GATT

Despite efforts at international coordination, the work on drawing up GSP schemes proceeded mainly at the national level. As a result each donor country eventually applied a somewhat different scheme and introduced it at a different time. This situation resulted from the fact that the GSP system did not entail contractual obligations under GATT rules: it was purely a 'matter of *ex gratia* grant by the (developed countries)'.[14]

One last problem remained before the implementation of the GSP could actually proceed. The MFN clause of the GATT provides that trade should be conducted on a non-discriminatory basis. A waiver of this clause had, however, already been granted in 1966 to Australia, which was permitted to introduce a system of preferences on imports of specified products from certain developing countries.[15] On a similar basis, the Contracting Parties to GATT voted a ten-year waiver from the MFN clause in June 1971. The next month, the European Community introduced its system of preferences and most countries of the Organization for Economic Cooperation and Development (OECD) followed suit soon afterwards. The United States finally introduced its own GSP programme in January 1976 after the Community had replaced reciprocal preferences in favour of the African associates which were introduced under the Yaoundé and Arusha agreements with non-reciprocal preferences under the first Lomé convention.[16] The United States had linked its agreement to the GSP to the removal of the discriminatory treatment of American exports by the Community's African associates compared with that accorded to the Community's own exports. This precondition was fulfilled by the agreement of the members of the Community to non-reciprocal preferences.

Since their original implementation, individual GSP schemes have been subject to pressures for change from both developing and developed countries. The main efforts of developing countries have been directed toward extending the scope of the schemes, while the developed countries have focussed their attention on limiting the access of particularly competitive developing countries to GSP benefits. The agreements relating to the framework for the conduct of world trade which were concluded in 1979 at the end of the Tokyo Round of multilateral trade negotiations addressed the concerns of both parties. The so-called 'enabling clause' provided the legal basis for the extension of GSP beyond its original ten-year period. It established an exception to the MFN clause and permitted departures from the obligation to extend equal treatment to all contracting parties in order to extend differential and more favourable treatment to developing countries. At the same time, however, the enabling clause envisaged that developing countries would participate more fully in the framework of rights and obligations of GATT as their economies progressively developed. In other words, it provides that individual developing countries might graduate successfully from special treatment, in general, and from the GSP in particular.

OUTLINE OF THE STUDY

The purpose of the present essay is to assess the successes and failures of the GSP in the light of its objectives. The focus will be limited to examining the GSP schemes of the European Community and the United States which, together, account for about 70 per cent of all OECD imports covered by GSP schemes.[17] Each chapter of the essay will analyze separately the European and the American schemes and will also compare them to each other. Chapter 2 provides a description of the main GSP schemes. The core of the study is Chapters 3, 4 and 5 which assess the economic effects of the European and American schemes. The concluding chapter reviews the findings and consider the future of the GSP.

NOTES AND REFERENCES

1. See Richard N. Gardner *Sterling-Dollar Diplomacy* (Oxford: Clarendon Press, 1956) for a discussion of the debate during World War II and thereafter.

2. By 'liberal' is meant a system in which stable and market-compatible trade policy instruments (namely, the tariff) are used and in which the general trend of trade policy is in a liberalizing direction. Non-discrimination was a major objective of the representatives of the United States, but on this point there was resistance in the United Kingdom where there was attachment to imperial preferences. This conflict may be seen as a harbinger of the many conflicts over discrimination and preferences that have occurred since World War II.

3. See Robert E. Baldwin, 'The Changing Nature of US Trade Policy Since World War II', in Baldwin and Anne O. Krueger (eds), *The Structure and Evolution of Recent US Trade Policy* (Chicago: University of Chicago Press, 1984), p. 10.

4. See Gardner, *op. cit.*, chapter 17.

5. See Kenneth Dam, *The GATT: Law and International Economic Organization* (Chicago and London: University of Chicago Press, 1970) p. 225.

6. For a discussion on GATT and the developing countries, see Robert E. Hudec, *Developing Countries in the GATT Legal System* (London: Trade Policy Research Centre, forthcoming); Anwar Hoda, *Gatt Reform and the Developing Countries*, Working Paper No. 7 (New Delhi: Indian Council for Research on International Economic Relations, 1983); Harry G. Johnson, *Economic Policies Toward Less Developed Countries* (Washington: Brookings Institution, 1967); Karin Kock, *International Trade Policy and the GATT* (Stockholm: Almqvist and Wiksell, 1969); and Martin Wolf, 'Two-edged Sword: Demands of Developing Countries and the Trading System', in Jagdish Bhagwati and John G. Ruggie (eds), *Power, Passions and Purpose: Prospects for North-South Negotiations*, (Cambridge, Mass: MIT Press, 1984), pp. 201-229.

7. The 'principal supplier' rule says that concessions on a particular product will normally be made by the largest exporter of that product (that is, the principal supplier) because it is the principal supplier who under the unconditional most-favoured-nation rule has the highest gain from, and consequently will give a greatest reciprocal counter-concession in return for, a concession on that product. Actually, the 'principal supplier' rule was simply a formal codification of an economic principle inherent in the nature of bilateral negotiations. See, Dam, *op. cit.*, pp. 61-62.

8. See *Trends in International Trade. Report by a Panel of Experts* (Geneva: GATT Secretariat, 1958).

9. See Dam, *op. cit.*, p. 230, who reports that of 4,400 tariff concessions made in the Dillon Round (the fifth GATT round which took place in 1961-62), only 160 were then considered of interest to the developing countries.

10. The account given here draws on Johnson *op. cit.*, and Tracy Murray, *Trade Preferences for Developing Countries* (New York: John Wiley, 1977).

11. See Johnson, *op. cit.*, p. 26.

12. See Raúl Prebisch, *Towards a New Trade Policy for Development* (New York: United Nations, 1964).

13. See US Congress, *The Future of United States Foreign Trade Policy*, hearings before the Sub-committee on Foreign Economic Policy of the Joint Economic Committee. 90th Congress, 1st Session, Vol. 1 (Washington: Government Printing Office, 1967), p. 79.

14. See Sidney Golt, *Developing Countries in the GATT System*, Thames Essay No. 13 (London: Trade Policy Research Centre, 1978), p. 26.

15. See Dam, *op. cit.*, p. 52.

16. The Lomé Convention is a successor of two earlier reciprocal agreements between the EEC-Six and eighteen Sub-Saharan African ex-colonies of France and Belgium (the so-called Yaoundé agreements of 1963 and 1969). In 1975, the Yaoundé agreements were adapted, after the first enlargement of the Community in 1973, into a non-reciprocal trade and aid convention (the Lomé Convention) originally covering 46 countries. The second Lomé Convention was signed in 1979 with 58 countries of the African, Caribbean and Pacific area (called ACP associates). The third convention was signed in December 1984 covering 65 ACP associates. The three conventions have established: (i) duty-free access for ACP-originating manufactures and most tropical

agricultural goods; (ii) financial assistance and, (iii) a stabilization scheme for primary export revenues of ACP associates.

17. For details on the other schemes of developed countries, see OECD, *The Generalised System of Preferences: Review of the First Decade* (Paris: OECD Secretariat, 1983).

Chapter 2

Nature and Coverage of Two GSP Schemes

THE PURPOSE of this chapter is to sketch the GSP schemes of the United States and the European Community. It is divided into three sections. The first section examines the scheme of the United States and the second the Community's scheme. The third section concludes with a brief comparison between the two.

GSP Scheme of the United States

The United States was the last among the developed countries to introduce a GSP scheme. This delay reflected the generally negative attitude toward preferences which had prevailed there. The opposition of both free-traders and protectionists, as well as the political nature of the American endorsement of the GSP, are reflected in the language of Title V of the 1974 Trade Act, which provides the guidelines for the American scheme. Section 501, which grants the President the authority to extend preferences, requires him to do so with due regard to:

(a) their effect on the economic development of developing countries;

(b) their likely impact on American producers; and

(c) the extent of similar preferences being granted by the other major developed countries.

Clearly point (a) was addressed to free-traders, who defend the view that a non-discriminatory reduction in MFN tariff rates would be more beneficial to the developing countries (and the world) than the GSP. Point (b) was directed at the protectionists who feared the impact of the scheme on American producers. Finally, point (c) clarified the foreign policy reasons for the American acceptance of the GSP.

The American GSP scheme is subject to a number of restrictions affecting its country coverage, product coverage, and extent of preferential treatment. Moreover, Section 505 of the 1974 Trade Act stated that the scheme was to terminate ten years after the date of its enactment, that is on 3 January 1985. Some changes to the system were made following a mandated report prepared on its first five years of operation. More changes were introduced by the Trade and Tariff Act of 1984, signed into law on 30 October 1984, which extended the American scheme for a further period ending on 4 July 1993.[1] The main part of this essay investigates the operation of the earlier GSP scheme. The changes introduced by the new legislation will be discussed in Chapters 5 and 6.

Section 502 of the 1974 Trade Act deals with the notion of a 'beneficiary developing country'. Instead of enumerating the developing countries that can benefit from the American GSP, section 502 outlines conditions which should guide the President in determining whether to designate a country as a 'beneficiary developing country'. These are (a) a request by the country to be so designated; (b) the level of economic development of the country; (c) whether or not the other major developed countries extend their GSP schemes to the country; and (d) the extent to which the country has assured the United States of equitable and reasonable access to its market and basic commodity resources.

Even if a country meets these four conditions, Section 502 specifies that the President shall not designate it as a beneficiary if:

    (i) it is a communist country;

    (ii) it participates in international commodity cartels such as the Organization of Petroleum Exporting Countries (OPEC);

(iii) if it affords preferences to another developed country which have a significant adverse effect on American commerce;

(iv) it has expropriated American property without compensation;

(v) it refuses to cooperate with the United States to prevent narcotics from entering the United States; and

(vi) it fails to recognize or enforce arbitration awards in favour of American citizens or firms.[2]

Except for the countries that fall within one of the above categories, all developing countries have been designated beneficiaries of the American GSP.[3]

Product Coverage

Although protectionist groups in the United States were not able to exclude the most competitive developing countries from GSP treatment, they did succeed in restricting the product coverage of the GSP. Section 503 of the 1974 Trade Act, which relates to the eligibility of products, lists the following import-sensitive products as ineligible for tariff preferences: (i) textile and apparel articles subject to textile agreements; (ii) watches; (iii) import-sensitive electronic articles; (iv) import-sensitive steel items; (v) footwear articles; (vi) import-sensitive glass products;[4] and (vii) any other articles which the President determines to be import-sensitive in the context of the GSP.

The regulations governing the administration of the GSP provide that any interested party may petition to have articles either removed from or added to the GSP list. Decisions are taken by the President based on investigations by the GSP Sub-committee of the Trade Policy Staff Committee.[5]

Limitations on Preferential Treatment

In order to prevent exports from non-beneficiary countries being shipped via beneficiary countries for the sole purpose of receiving GSP treatment, donor countries have instituted a set of rules of origin. In the United States, duty-free treatment for GSP-eligible products applies only if (i) a product is imported directly from a beneficiary developing country into the United States and (ii) the sum of the cost or value of materials produced in the beneficiary country plus the direct costs of processing equals at least 35 per cent of the value of the product.[6] Although these rules are primarily intended to ensure the proper operation of the GSP, they also might serve a protectionist purpose in certain instances. In particular, they might deter American multinational corporations, in some cases, from responding to GSP margins by transferring production to beneficiary developing countries.[7]

In addition, Section 504 of the 1974 Trade Act establishes competitive need limitations according to which a beneficiary developing country loses duty-free treatment under the GSP for a particular product if its exports to the United States exceeds (i) 50 per cent of the value of the total American imports of the product;[8] or (ii) a certain dollar value adjusted annually in accordance with the growth of the United States gross national product.[9] The loss of preferences takes effect on 30 March of each year.[10] Reinstatement of GSP treatment may be considered if American imports of the particular product from the excluded country fall below the competitive-need limitations in subsequent years. Hence, during any given year (from 30 March to the following 29 March), imports of a product from a beneficiary country enter the United States either entirely duty-free under the GSP or entirely at the MFN rate.[11]

It is often emphasized that competitive-need limitations are designed to reserve the benefits of the programme for less competitive producers in not-so-advanced developing countries. It should also be recognized, however, that these limitations are mainly the result of domestic protectionist pressures.

GSP Scheme of the European Community

The implementation of the European Community's GSP scheme has undergone gradual changes since its inception in

1971. Its fundamental principles, however, have remained the same:

(i) full tariff exemption for most of the exports of semi-manufactures and manufactures from beneficiaries subject to various preconditions and within certain product- and country-specific limits which are fixed annually and

(ii) a full or partial tariff exemption for some processed agricultural products under restrictions that are similar to those for semi-manufactures and manufactures.

After the number of countries in the Community had increased to 9 in the early 1970s, the new members, United Kingdom, Denmark and Ireland abandoned their national schemes and converted to the Community scheme on 1 January 1974.

Country Coverage

In selecting countries for GSP status, the European Community considered Group of 77 membership as its point of departure (the so-called self-selection process). Thus, preferential treatment under the GSP was denied to Taiwan and Israel but granted to Yugoslavia. In addition to this group, Romania and the People's Republic of China were included in the list of beneficiaries in 1974 and 1980 respectively. For cotton textiles and substitutes the Community confined beneficiary status to those developing countries that were contracting parties to the Long Term Arrangement Regarding Trade in Cotton Textiles (LTA). After 1980 the Community offered preferential treatment for products subject to the Multi-fibre Agreement (MFA) only when bilateral 'voluntary' export restraints on those products had been agreed with the Community.[12] In 1980, 21 countries and dependent territories (including Romania) plus nine least developed countries apart from the African, Caribbean and Pacific associates (ACP group) were granted preferential treatment for MFA products.[13] Applications from dependent territories were approved if their customs administrations were authorized to issue certificates of origin.

In 1983, 125 independent countries were GSP beneficiaries. Sixty three of them also enjoyed special preferences under the ACP agreement. In addition, nine Mediterranean countries received preferences under bilateral agreements. These countries have the option of claiming preferential treatment under whichever system is more favourable to them. In most cases, these special preferences have been at least equivalent to the preferences under the GSP arrangements in respect of exports of manufactures; they have been more favourable in respect of agricultural products. Special rules introduced in 1977 provide additional preferences for least developed countries which do not belong to the ACP group. For these countries, the GSP product range has been extended to products like raw coffee and cocoa beans. Furthermore, safeguards like ceilings and other quantitative limitations under the GSP have been liberalized for the least developed countries.

Product Coverage

Only a few items of manufactures and semi-manufactures are excluded from GSP treatment in the European Community. In formulating these exclusions, the Community took account of the interests of competing suppliers from the ACP associates. About 96 per cent of all manufactured and semi-manufactured products have been within the GSP from the beginning. By contrast, although the Community raised the number of processed agricultural products covered by the GSP from 145 in 1971 to 338 in 1983, this represents only 74 per cent of all items exported. The greatest improvements in product coverage were achieved between 1975 and 1977 when Asian Commonwealth countries were compensated for the loss, in the United Kingdom market, of Commonwealth preferences which expired in 1978.

Limitations on Preferential Treatment

In addition to a general escape clause for processed agricultural products, which is intended mainly to protect the export interests of competing ACP suppliers, a considerable number of *a priori* limitations exist for manufactures and semi-manufactures.

For each GSP item a ceiling is calculated annually on the basis of past trade flows. The sum of all ceilings indicates the annual 'GSP offer'. In practice, however, this offer is by no means available in the same way for all products. In principle, imports exceeding the ceilings face the MFN tariff, but ceilings can be enforced either automatically, on a discretionary basis, or not at all, depending on the category into which a particular product falls. The European Community divides imported products into three categories, non-sensitive, semi-sensitive and sensitive, depending on the extent to which imports from GSP beneficiaries are likely to threaten domestic production and employment in the member states.

Ceilings on non-sensitive products are not published and, although duties could be reimposed under a general safeguard clause, no member country has in fact ever requested this. In practice, duty-free treatment for non-sensitive items is open-ended provided that administrative conditions (origin rules and so forth) are met and the importers apply for GSP treatment.

The next category, the so-called semi-sensitive list, existed until 1981. It included imports of borderline items which were expected eventually to disrupt the internal market of the European Community; such items were, therefore, placed under permanent surveillance. Ceilings for such products were discretionary, but imports beyond a certain level frequently faced MFN treatment at the request of member states. Consequently, there was a considerable amount of uncertainty as to the sort of tariff treatment which imports of items in this category might receive. The category was abandoned in 1981 for all industrial products except textiles. Since most of the formerly semi-sensitive items were put in the sensitive category, which is the more restrictive, the surveillance was not relaxed, but increased.

For sensitive items, which comprise goods that compete strongly with domestic substitutes, ceilings take the form of tariff quotas and imports that exceed a quota automatically face MFN treatment. In addition, a further restriction is introduced. The tariff quota for each sensitive item is divided into fixed shares for each member state, so that GSP imports into a member state whose share is exhausted are only possible via another member state whose share is not yet used up. These indirect imports cause additional costs and are only profitable if the additional costs are lower than the tariff saving. In practice, indirect imports are made frequently, not only because of the GSP, but also because of short-term adjustments to changing market conditions. In fact, the free circulation of goods within the Community makes member state shares costly to administer and ultimately useless. Since the mid-1970s, a Community reserve allows for some inter-member state re-allocation of import shares.

A further limitation is the rule that imposes 'butoir' on each exporter, a limitation which is based on one of the essential perceptions of GSP administrators, that is 'differentiation' among countries. The 'butoir' simply limits the share of the pie (the strictly limited GSP offer, particularly in sensitive items) that can be received by the most competitive suppliers, the aim being to guarantee some share for the smaller suppliers or the least developed developing countries. Up to 1980 the *butoir*, which denoted the maximum share of a ceiling which an individual beneficiary could use, ranged between 50 per cent for non-sensitive items and 15 per cent for so-called 'hybrid' products.

The latter category included some products where a few major suppliers frequently took up the normal *butoir*. In these products the European Community pretended to defend preferential access for the majority of GSP beneficiaries against the few agressive exporters by imposing very restrictive tariff quotas. In practice, however, the *butoir* was often exceeded before the MFN tariff was reimposed. This happened because of time-lags in the processing of information between the member states and the European Commission.

Since 1981 tariff quotas and *butoirs* have been combined in a new sub-category of very sensitive items, in which some developing countries which are regarded as very competitive with domestic producers have each been granted identical tariff quotas, not as a percentage share but in absolute amounts. These amounts are again sub-divided among member states and are strictly obligatory. Other countries which receive GSP treatment and also export very sensitive items face discretionary ceilings as do all GSP beneficiaries in another sub-category of somewhat less sensitive items.[14] In both cases tariffs may be reimposed *ad hoc* at the request of member states.

Preferences are by no means automatically granted by the customs authorities of the importing country. Customs authorities are bound by origin rules, which are typically restrictive for goods where the interests of domestic producers are considerable, as well as by the requirement that goods be shipped directly from the country of origin.[15] The relevant documents have to be filled in by the exporter and certified by authorities in the exporting country. If, as happened in the case of the People's Republic of China in 1980 and partly again in 1981, the correct origin certificate is not available, GSP treatment will not be granted. All the other safeguard provisions then become redundant.

Complex administrative constraints are a natural consequence of the discriminatory treatment implicit in the GSP. Thus, in order to apply the notion that exporting countries should be divided into those who 'need' duty-free market access and others who do not need it, origin rules are used. By their very nature, GSP-induced export incentives and origin controls are interdependent. Thus, generous incentives to export provoke both the faking of invoices and the shipping of products through those GSP beneficiary countries which have not yet 'eaten their piece of the pie', with the least possible transformation in such countries, in order to obtain the benefit of preferences. Stricter origin controls will follow automatically and these will, in turn, result in an unproductive use of resources and a decline in the attractiveness of preferences for those countries which have a comparative advantage in producing particular categories of goods.

COMPARISON OF THE SCHEMES

In theory, the European Community's scheme is more comprehensive than that of the United States. The Community's preference scheme applies to all members of the Group of 77 and covers all manufactured products as well as many agricultural products. The American scheme does not grant beneficiary treatment in a blanket fashion; it is rather a matter of the fulfillment of specific conditions by individual countries. Moreover, the American scheme excludes certain categories of manufactured products and has a less extensive coverage of agricultural products than in the Community.

Nevertheless, in practice the European Community's GSP scheme could well be less effective than the American scheme, for two major reasons. First, under the American scheme, all products that actually receive GSP treatment, enter the American market duty-free and there are no quantitative limits during any given year. The Community, however, grants duty-free treatment to all manufactures but only to about 20 per cent of agricultural products with other items benefitting from partial reduction of MFN duties. Second, and more important, limitations on preferential treatment and other administrative rules are much more extensive in the Community scheme than in the American GSP. The system of limitations and rules is also much more complex in the case of the Community. In part, this is due to the fact that it comprises twelve countries, each of which has its own particular interests to further in the course of formulating a common Community position.

To conclude, both the European Community and the American schemes fall far short of granting generalized preferences. In the Community's case this is because wide country- and product-coverage is offset by ceilings and other administrative rules which are extensive. In the American case, rules and limitations are fewer, but country- and product-coverage are more limited.

NOTES AND REFERENCES

1. The operation of the GSP during its first five years is reviewed in *Report to the Congress on the First Five Years' Operation of the United States Generalized System of Preferences (GSP)*, Committee on Ways and Means, US House of Representatives, 96th Congress, 2nd session (Washington: Government Printing Office, 1980). A further review is provided in US Senate, Committee on Finance, *Renewal of the Generalized System of Preferences*. 98th Congress, 2nd session (Washington: Government Printing Office, 1984).

2. The last three conditions may be waived if the President determines that doing so is in the national economic interest of the United States.

3. Hence, the developing countries which are non-beneficiaries of the American GSP are: the People's Republic of China and other communist countries, except Romania and Yugoslavia; OPEC members, except Ecuador, Indonesia and Venezuela which were designated as beneficiaries with effect from 30 March 1980; Greece and Spain which, prior to their accession to the Community granted preferences to the Community; (Portugal became a beneficiary on 1 October 1976, following its decision to reduce preferences for EEC countries on products of interest to the United States but ceased to be so after it joined the Community on 1 January 1986); a few countries which have expropriated property owned by citizens of the United States without compensation (People's Democratic Republic of Yemen, Uganda up to 30 March 1980, and Ethiopia since that date).

4. Section 503 does not specify which electronic, steel and glass articles are import-sensitive. The precise determination is made by the President, in consultation with various parties, on the basis of the probable economic effects of GSP treatment on domestic producers of similar products.

5. See *Annual GSP Changes*, Office of the United States Trade Representative, (Washington: 1982), mimeographed, and *A Guide to the U.S. Generalized System of Preferences (GSP)*, Office of the United

States Trade Representative, (Washington: 1983).

6. The American GSP contains provisions of cumulative origin for beneficiary countries which are members of designated regional economic associations.

7. This argument is developed by Murray, *op. cit.*, pp. 89-92.

8. This limitation does not apply to certain products which the Trade Policy Staff Committee considers are not produced in the United States. For their list, see Office of the United States Trade Representative, 1983, *op. cit.* A *de minimis* provision, effective since 30 March 1980, allows the President to waive this limitation in cases where total American imports of a product do not exceed a certain dollar value to be adjusted annually; it was $US1 million in 1980.

9. The value was set at $US25 million for 1975. It has grown from $US26.6 million for 1976 to $US57.7 million for 1984.

10. As from 1980, the date for implementing annual competitive-need exclusions and changes in the GSP product list was changed from 60 to 90 days after the end of the calendar year.

11. Obviously the only GSP-covered imports receiving GSP treatment are those for which preferences are requested and rules of origin are fulfilled. Also, it should be noted that during a calendar year (from 1 January to 31 December) some imports would be duty-free and some would be charged at the MFN rate if a change in GSP treatment occurred on 30 March.

12. The link between export restraint agreements and GSP treatment is strictly applied. The Republic of Korea, which was late in signing the bilateral agreement under MFA III by a few days, was subjected to the 'penalty' that its textile exports received preferential treatment only from 1 February 1983. Since most of the importers of Korean textiles were not aware of this, they had to pay the duties after declaring the imports in early January, whereas a few well-informed importers waited until February and then collected the 'information rent'.

13. It is typical of the GSP practice in the Community that the Commission calculated a 'competitiveness' indicator for preferential treatment of MFA products by multiplying the GNP *per capita* of a beneficiary by its share of Community textile imports from all beneficiaries. The higher this indicator, the lower is the duty-free share of the beneficiary's textile exports to the Community. Hong Kong was at the top according to this indicator and its quota of duty-free exports in 1980 amounted to only 2 per cent of its 1977 textile exports to the Community. Sri Lanka whose exports to the

Community in 1977 were 0.04 per cent of those of Hong Kong was allowed 65 per cent of its exports duty-free in 1980.

15. See Ann Weston, 'Who is More Preferred? An Analysis of the New Generalized System of Preferences', in Christopher Stevens (ed.), *EEC and the Third World. A Survey. 2. Hunger in the World* (London: Overseas Development Institute and Institute for Development Studies, 1982), pp. 73-86.

16. An example will illustrate the restrictive nature of origin rules. To qualify for GSP treatment a radio or television set requires, first, that the import content does not exceed 40 per cent of the total value, second that at least 50 per cent in value of the intermediate parts originate in the country seeking preference and, third, that all the transistors also originate in that country. The last provision, especially, has disqualified many products of South East Asian countries from GSP treatment since, because of large economies of scale, they import transistors from Japan and the United States. It seems obvious that the Community included this provision with full knowledge of this division of labour in order to impose a brake on duty-free imports of radios and television sets.

Chapter 3

Trade Effects of the Main GSP Schemes

THE PURPOSE of this and the following two chapters is to review the evidence on the economic effects of the GSP schemes of the United States and the European Community.

This chapter will briefly examine first of all the theoretical basis of the schemes and ways in which their effect can be measured. The trade effects of the American and the Community schemes will then be considered before a general comparison of the trade effects is made in the final section. Chapter 4 will consider the distribution of the benefits from the GSP schemes and Chapter 5, the consequences of the administrative rules on the potential benefits of the schemes.

THEORY AND MEASUREMENT

Conceptually, a preferential tariff reduction (like the GSP) is similar to the formation of a customs union. Both give rise to the same static effects, often described as trade creation and trade diversion. The trade creation effect corresponds to the displacement of domestic production in the donor country in favour of imports from beneficiary countries. The trade diversion effect pertains to the substitution by the donor country of imports from preferred suppliers in place of imports from non-preferred countries. Beneficiary developing countries attach more significance to the sum of both the trade creation and trade diversion effects, which reflects the total impact of preferences on their exports. This sum is often referred to as gross trade creation. According to the theory of customs unions, trade creation increases the welfare of the donor country, since resources will move from inefficient import-competing sectors into more productive uses. However, trade diversion implies a welfare loss, since imports are diverted from more efficient to less efficient suppliers.

As already indicated in Chapter 1, the GSP has two distinct components: (i) a reduction of tariffs and (ii) preferential treatment for some suppliers. The first component should give rise to trade creation, while the second is likely to result in trade diversion. It could be argued that one of the objectives of the GSP would be realised if there has been more trade creation than trade diversion. The impact of the GSP is, of course, likely to be different for each product and for each donor country. As far as products are concerned, the relative magnitude of the two effects depends upon whether a product competes more with domestic producers in the donor country or with suppliers in non-beneficiary countries. It is easier, however, to predict the relative magnitude of trade creation and trade diversion in respect of a particular donor-country market.

In the European Community, the scope for trade diversion is not likely to be very large because, during the 1970s, the Community negotiated free trade arrangements in manufactures with almost all its major trading partners (except Japan and the United States). As a consequence the preferential margins of GSP beneficiaries against non-beneficiaries were reduced and so were the effects of trade diversion. The situation is different in the United States. Most of its imports are subject to the MFN tariff, so the existence of GSP preferences should provide a greater opportunity for trade diversion.

Empirically, several methods can be used to estimate the trade creation and trade diversion effects of preferential trading arrangements.[1] Among these, a distinction must be made between *ex ante* and *ex post* methods. The former seek to estimate the effects of preferential tariff reductions in advance of their implementation. In addition to estimates of tariff reductions, *ex ante* methods also require estimates of domestic and foreign supply elasticities as well as of domestic and cross-price import demand elasticities. On the other hand, *ex post* methods seek to isolate the effect of preferential arrangements on actual trade flows from the effects of changes in other determinants of trade. The next two sections, will seek to summarize estimates which have been derived from the use of different methods, concerning the trade effects of the GSP schemes in the United States and the European Community.

One *ex post* method uses data for actual trade flows after the introduction of preferences which are then compared to an *anti-monde* (that is hypothetical trade flows corresponding to a situation of unchanged tariffs); the difference is the tariff effect. Obviously the crucial element is the construction of the *anti-monde*. One way to construct this is to compare market shares before and after a tariff change. Several different market shares can be compared such as (i) that of beneficiary and non-beneficiary countries in a donor market; (ii) that of beneficiary countries in donor versus non-donor markets; or (iii) that of GSP-eligible and non-eligible products in a donor market.[2]

A second method introduces a tariff variable into the analysis and then estimates statistically the relationship between trade flows and tariff preferences.[3] This can be done with a so called cross-sectional gravity model which explains exports from beneficiary and non-beneficiary countries to donor and non-donor countries respectively.[4] If a model is constructed using data for the years before and after the introduction of a GSP scheme, then a change in the co-efficient of the tariff variable indicates (if it is significantly positive) a growth in exports from beneficiary to donor countries. The major advantage of this approach is that it provides a test of the statistical significance of tariff effects. On the other hand, like *ex post* methods in general, it will only give reliable estimates for periods during which the trade effects of tariff changes are relatively large compared to the effects of other factors which might not be included in the model.

In *ex ante* methods, trade creation is measured as the product of three terms: (i) the price elasticity of demand for imports, (ii) the initial value of imports from beneficiaries before the introduction of the GSP, and (iii) the percentage change in the price of imports to the consumer caused by the tariff cut. Various assumptions on cross-price demand elasticities are then made so that trade diversion can be derived from trade creation and market shares.[5]

A further method of measurement consists of using the *ex ante* measure of trade creation described above and a measure of trade diversion based on estimates of *ex post* elasticities of substitution between beneficiary and non-beneficiary sources.

As explained in Chapter 2, for various reasons under both the American and the Community GSP schemes not all the imports which are eligible for preferential treatment actually obtain it. For example, tariff quotas may be exhausted, countries may be excluded because of the competitive-need clause, imports may fail to meet origin rules or countries may simply fail to apply for preferential treatment. Therefore, if a variant of the methods outlined briefly above is used, the percentage change in the price of imports might be estimated on the basis of the actual preference margin (APM) rather than the theoretical preference margin (TPM).[6] The theoretical preference margin is the relevant MFN tariff; the actual margin is the theoretical margin times the proportion of eligible trade that actually enters a donor country GSP duty-free.

TRADE EFFECTS OF THE AMERICAN
   SCHEME

Various studies have attempted to estimate the trade effects of the American GSP scheme. All of the methods outlined earlier have been used, with the exception of the last one. The *first method* was used in a recent study by the United States International Trade Commission which examined import and consumption figures for the period 1978-81 disaggregated into 650 commodity areas.[7] Within each of these areas, three indicators were computed: the trend of imports subject to GSP treatment relative to total imports; the trend of total imports relative to total consumption; and the trend of imports subject to GSP treatment relative to total consumption. For the commodity groups in which the trend in all three ratios was found to be positive, it was considered that the GSP could have played a significant role in bringing about increased import penetration of the American market. The Commission therefore, undertook an in-depth study in order to gauge the factors which caused this increased penetration.

It was found that in only twelve of the 650 commodity groups studied had there been a significant increase in import penetration as a result of the GSP scheme. It concluded that the absence of significant import growth in the vast majority of product areas was the result of the substitution of imports which obtained GSP treatment for imports from other developed countries not eligible for GSP treatment. In other words, the Commission found little evidence of trade creation but strong indications of trade diversion. No quantitative evaluation of these trade effects is provided in the Commission's study.

The *second method*, which involves the statistical analysis of the impact of GSP preferences on trade flows, was recently used in a study by Professor André Sapir and Dr Lars Lundberg.[8] These authors formulate different models which explain international trade flows on the basis of a set of factors that include tariff preferences. Professor Sapir and Dr Lundberg use cross-section regression models which explain trade flows and market shares either for particular products across countries (the cross-country model) or for particular countries across products (the cross-product model). The models were estimated for 1975 (the last year before the introduction of the American GSP) and 1979 (the latest year for which the required data were available at the time of writing).

The *cross-country* model of Professor Sapir and Dr Lundberg contains a variable measuring the actual preference margin by product and country and the main determinants of trade flows from different countries to the United States such as: (i) the distance of each country from the United States, (ii) its total manufactured exports, (iii) its physical and human capital endowment, and (iv) the relative importance of American direct investment. The model was estimated separately for 15 products identified in earlier studies as having potentially large GSP effects.[9] The regression results indicate a significant GSP effect in about half of the cases studied.[10] The authors note that the effectiveness of the GSP programme seems to be associated with products enjoying large preferential margins and countries which were already major suppliers of particular products in the United States before the introduction of the GSP. The latter factor might be attributable to the fact that Professor Sapir and Dr Lundberg's study related only to an extremely short period of time.

In their *cross-product* model, Professor Sapir and Dr Lundberg specify a variable measuring the actual preference margin by product and country as well as variables indicating the physical and human capital intensities of the individual products. The model was estimated over three aggregates: (i) beneficiary countries, (ii) non-beneficiary countries, and (iii) all countries. In each case, the estimation was made on a sample of 208 products. The estimates of the coefficient of the preference variables indicated the presence of (net) trade creation as well as gross trade creation. A quantitative estimate was made of these two magnitudes as well as of the amount of trade diversion.[11] The results confirmed the importance of the pre-1976 market share of beneficiary countries in explaining their ability to take advantage of the GSP. The coefficients of the cross-product model were then used to compute an estimate of the GSP effects. Out of the 208 products in their sample, Professor Sapir and Dr Lundberg found 33 for which there was a positive gross trade creation effect. The total effect amounted to $US930 million, of which 95 per cent was accounted for by the top 20 products. In general, the results indicated that trade creation was about two-and-half times larger than trade diversion. This runs counter the conclusion from the United States International Trade Commission study described earlier.

The *third method* was first used by Professor Robert Baldwin and Professor Tracy Murray in order to estimate the impact of the GSP in the United States, the European Community and Japan.[12] The *ex ante* trade expansion effects estimated by these authors were based on 1971 trade flows and theoretical preference margins. They estimated trade expansion amounting to nearly 30 per cent of the 1971 trade flows. According to the Baldwin-Murray estimates, 80 per cent of this expansion would be accounted for by trade creation.

In their study, Professor Sapir and Dr Lundberg had also used this method to estimate the trade creation effects of the GSP, but they used 1979 trade flows as well as both actual and theoretical preference margins. Their estimates indicate a hypothetical decrease in American imports from beneficiary countries that would have occurred in 1979 if preferences had been eliminated. For all GSP-eligible products, Professor Sapir and Dr Lundberg calculated a total trade creation effect of $US2.2 billion when the theoretical preference margin was used. On the other hand, the effect obtained by using the actual preference margin was only $US1.3 billion. The difference between the figures derived from the theoretical and the actual margins of preference is an estimate of the impact of GSP limitations on eligible products. The trade creation effect computed with actual preference margins amounted to 21 per cent of GSP duty-free imports by the United States in 1979.

TRADE EFFECTS OF THE COMMUNITY SCHEME

As explained in the second chapter, the Community scheme makes extensive use of discretionary tariff ceilings and obligatory tariff quotas to limit benefits under the scheme. Imports exceeding the limits may face or will face MFN tariffs.

If limits are obligatory, as in the case of tariff quotas, there will be no effective price incentive at the margin and hence no additional trade will arise from the GSP. In this case, tariff quotas are 'closed'. Trade effects can only occur if the quotas are 'open-ended', that is if they are higher than the actual volume of imports but in this case, the limitation on imports will be ineffective.[13]

Rolf Langhammer has measured changes in import-consumption ratios in the Community and United States/Canada[14] between 1972 and 1975.[15] Although the study indicates that import penetration ratios in manufacturing are similar in both areas, the validity of such a comparison may be questioned because of other divergences in the general demand patterns of the two areas and particularly during the period covered. Any conclusion drawn from the comparison should therefore be tentative, especially in view of the short period used for comparison.

The results show that imports from non-beneficiaries as a proportion of apparent consumption increased in the Community more than in the United States/Canada. This is contrary to what would be expected under an effective GSP. It suggests a negative trade diversion in that the less favourable treatment they received apparently did not deter non-beneficiaries from penetrating the Community market. The same effect was also noticeable in the American market but to a less marked degree. Thus, the estimated GSP effect was inconsistent with the expectation of positive trade creation and diversion.

The trade flow method was employed by Professor Sapir to estimate the GSP effects for the European Community. He used Standard International Trade Classification (SITC) data for the period 1967 and 1978.[16] The conclusions of the study were that dummy variables which reflected the GSP status of an exporting country in bilateral trade flows were statistically significant only in 1973 and 1974. Somewhat better results were achieved for disaggregated trade flows in two SITC categories: 7 (machinery and transport equipment) and 8 (miscellaneous manufactured articles).

This method of analysis was also used by Dr Langhammer for the period 1978-80 with some minor modifications. In his study, however, Dr Langhammer used total Brussels Tariff Nomenclature (BTN) import data and included only those manufactures which were subject to GSP treatment. The data were disaggregated by sensitivity categories to test the hypothesis that the beneficiary status produced larger export growth in non-sensitive than in sensitive items. The results rejected the hypothesis.

In general, these studies indicated that exports to the Community from developed countries, which did not receive GSP preferential treatment, were growing faster at the end of the 1970s than the Community's imports from the major GSP beneficiary countries. There are several factors which could explain this result:

(i) the free trade arrangements in manufactures between the Community and former European Free Trade Association (EFTA) countries;

(ii) the importance of trade between neighbours in Europe,

(iii) the positive impact of high income levels, both in exporting and importing countries on bilateral trade flows fostering intra-industry specialization,

(iv) the quantitative restrictions in standardized and labour-intensive consumer goods facing successful developing country suppliers on European markets; and

(v) the rather limited range of products of developing-country suppliers compared to the wide range of products in the trade between developed countries.

In the Baldwin-Murray study already referred to, the authors estimated the trade creation effects for manufactured products of the preferential treatment under the GSP arrangements.[17] On the basis of imports into the Community in 1971, Professor Baldwin and Professor Murray estimated trade creation effects of 22-25 per cent. Their results are, however, open to question.

First, the data used were inadequate in the sense that until 1973 the only data available were for imports *eligible* for preferential treatment. Trade in items that actually *received* GSP duty-free treatment could not be identified until 1973 when the Community began to record separately imports which received GSP treatment. The authors of this study simply assumed that all imports of GSP products from GSP beneficiaries would receive GSP treatment except for those items where the ceiling or tariff quota was exceeded. This assumption is likely to lead to an upward bias in the estimates.

Second, the estimates of trade creation made by Professor Baldwin and Professor Murray hold only on the assumptions of (i) an average GSP margin of about 10 percentage points and (ii) an average price elasticity of demand of about -2.5.[18] Only about one-third of the imports which are covered by the GSP arrangements, however, actually benefit from the tariff cuts. This ought to be taken into account in the calculation of trade creation and if it is, then Baldwin and Murray's estimate of trade creation effects in the Community would be reduced to about 8 per cent.

Third, Professor Baldwin and Professor Murray did not estimate separately elasticities of substitution for imports from GSP beneficiaries and non-beneficiaries to obtain estimates of trade diversion. Instead they simply assumed these elasticities to be equal to the elasticities of substitution between imports from beneficiaries and domestic production in the Community. Under this assumption trade diversion becomes trade creation weighted by the ratio between imports from non-beneficiaries and domestic production. While this assumption might facilitate estimation, it needs to be subjected to empirical verification.

Dr Langhammer, on the other hand, has estimated elasticities of substitution for Community imports from GSP beneficiaries and non-beneficiaries.[19] Import unit values and quantities were used in the estimates because of the lack of market price data. Since the estimates are based on individual non-sensitive GSP items, however, instead of on baskets of goods, the shortcomings of this approach would seem to be less serious.[20]

The estimate, in fact, reveals a theoretically plausible and statistically significant elasticity of substitution (-1.10) between Community imports from beneficiaries and non-beneficiaries according to the change in relative prices which occurred between 1970-72, when the preferences were introduced. This means that a ten per cent reduction in the relative prices of imports from beneficiaries because of the average preference margin would have resulted in an eleven per cent increase in import quantities from beneficiaries at the expense of import quantities from non-beneficiaries.

The crucial question still remains whether this empirical observation is a consequence of the introduction of GSP preferences. In view of the shortcomings (lack of data on market prices, possible product heterogeneity, overlap with simultaneous price changes other than tariff changes) scepticism is justified. As the observed elasticity seems to be rather small in view of the two-year period, so is trade diversion. In general, however, this result may hold for the Community, which has established extensive free trade arrangements in manufactures with the EFTA countries, thus leaving the United States and Japan as the major non-beneficiaries. Since the overlap between the manufactured exports of these two countries and those of the GSP beneficiaries is likely to be low, given their different resource endowments, it may be argued that the trade expansion effects of the Community GSP scheme, such as they are, are based primarily on trade creation.

COMPARISON OF THE TRADE EFFECTS

In general, the findings suggest a larger impact of the GSP arrangements on American imports from developing countries than on Community imports from developing countries. This is supported by the extent to which imports subject to the GSP actually received preferential treatment in both trading areas. Table 3.1 shows GSP trade figures for the United States;

between 1976-81 about 50 per cent of imports of GSP-covered products entered the market duty-free, whereas, in 1983, only about one quarter of beneficiary exports of GSP items to the Community received preferential treatment (Table 3.2). This means that the majority of Community imports of the relevant goods were denied GSP treatment because of limitations and administrative rules.

TABLE 3.1

US Imports: Total, MFN-Dutiable, and GSP Coverage
($US billion)

	1976	1977	1978	1979	1980	1981	1982	1983
From the world								
Total	119.5	145.5	170.7	210.0	245.0	260.0	n.a.	n.a.
MFN-dutiable	86.2	106.2	125.3	n.a.	n.a.	n.a.	n.a.	n.a.
From all developing countries								
Total	55.0	70.2	75.9	96.2	119.1	120.3	n.a.	n.a.
MFN-dutiable	45.6	58.0	62.0	n.a.	n.a.	n.a.	n.a.	n.a.
From all GSP beneficiaries								
Total	28.1	34.7	41.4	51.2	63.5	68.5	n.a.	n.a.
MFN-dutiable	20.9	25.4	31.4	38.2	53.8	n.a.	65.9	n.a.
GSP eligible trade	6.5	7.7	9.7	11.7	14.3	16.9	17.4	22.6
Exclusions								
50% limit	(0.7)	(0.8)	(1.0)	n.a.	n.a.	n.a.	n.a.	n.a.
dollar limit	(1.2)	(2.0)	(2.2)	n.a.	n.a.	n.a.	n.a.	n.a.
rules of origin and other[a]	(1.4)	(1.0)	(1.3)	(1.6)	(1.4)	n.a.	n.a.	n.a.
GSP duty-free trade	3.2	3.9	5.2	6.2	7.3	8.4	8.4	10.8

SOURCES: Office of the US Trade Representative and UNCTAD.
[a]Including the absence of request for GSP coverage.
n.a. means not available.

In the United States, it is mainly the competitive-need criteria that prevents importers from using the scheme more extensively. Importers in the Community, on the other hand, have to face tariff quotas and ceilings in sensitive and semi-sensitive products and this explains the extremely low share of GSP utilization in these categories. In the case of the open-ended, non-sensitive products, it is the origin rules which seem to be of great importance in limiting imports. The considerably higher number of ceiling limitations and greater degree of complexity of the Community scheme, which seems to act as a barrier in itself, tend, therefore, to outweigh the broader country and product coverage of the Community's GSP scheme.

The extent to which imports which receive GSP treatment would be stimulated by the GSP tariff preferences depends on the depth of tariff cuts and the price elasticities of demand. Actual preference margins in the Community ranged between about 15 per cent for sensitive textiles and 7 per cent for agricultural products compared to an average of about 5 per cent for all products in the United States (see Chapter 4). These higher incentives for increased trade in the Community, however, are to a large extent made ineffective. This is because strict tariff quotas put a brake on additional imports of precisely those goods where the initial tariff levels and hence preference margins are high. Viewed against the very low percentages of imports which receive GSP treatment in the total of GSP-eligible items (below 10 per cent in many years for sensitive textiles, Table 3.2) it might be said that the limitations have nearly the same effect as a full exclusion of sensitive products such as in the American scheme.

EXPORT-ORIENTED INVESTMENTS AND
GSP RESTRICTIONS

One of the potential dynamic effects of tariff preference schemes is their impact on investment. Although tariff preferences may influence investment decisions at the margin, they are certainly not the only, or even the main, determinant. Any attempt to quantify the marginal contribution of tariff preference schemes by survey interview methods is not likely to be very fruitful since the numerous quantitative and qualitative aspects cannot be made equivalent and comparable

TABLE 3.2

Percentage Share of GSP-receiving Imports[a] in GSP-covered Imports[b] of the European Community, 1978-83

	Year	Sensitive industrial products (except textiles)	Semi-sensitive industrial products (except textiles)[c]	Non-sensitive industrial products (except textiles)	Sensitive textiles	Semi-sensitive textiles[d]	Non-sensitive textiles	Sensitive agricultural products[e]	Semi-sensitive agricultural products[f]	Non-sensitive agricultural products	Total agricultural and manufactured products
European Community	1978	14.9	29.1	31.2	7.1	49.8	65.0	25.3	31.1	40.6	26.8
	1979	12.4	40.1	33.7	8.8	63.2	62.9	42.5	35.2	18.4	26.2
	1980	16.6	40.8	34.3	11.7	50.4	71.0	47.9	20.1	38.2	30.9
	1981	38.2	-	36.2	9.5	37.9	71.3	34.5	44.1	44.1	32.8
	1982	35.0	-	31.9	9.7	43.8	77.0	30.8	7.9	43.0	30.7
	1983	24.6	-	25.1	14.6	-	77.9	26.5	8.3	37.2	24.6
West Germany	1978	14.8	42.9	57.1	5.3	70.4	64.9	40.5	79.0	56.3	36.5
	1979	11.5	46.1	57.0	4.2	71.8	57.7	37.9	74.4	17.5	29.9
	1980	10.6	46.5	54.0	6.1	54.4	81.3	33.1	20.2	52.2	32.8
	1981	39.5	-	51.2	7.6	43.2	69.5	34.0	52.9	52.9	34.6
	1982	28.7	-	51.4	8.1	53.6	71.4	36.3	7.1	50.4	31.9
	1983	37.1	-	45.5	16.5	-	78.6	30.1	7.3	50.7	33.9
France	1978	8.7	24.0	20.8	9.6	42.8	31.1	2.9	7.7	24.0	19.1
	1979	8.5	15.8	22.4	10.2	64.5	38.3	2.7	nil	14.3	16.2

France—cont. 1980	7.9	6.9	21.7	11.7	56.3	43.8	2.9	nil	25.5	14.9
1981	12.2	-	23.9	12.5	44.5	48.2	4.2	41.7	41.7	20.3
1982	29.2	-	14.5	12.7	51.2	52.4	3.9	nil	40.9	23.1
1983	4.1	-	5.2	10.6	-	28.4	5.2	nil	14.4	6.7
Italy 1978	8.5	16.4	17.1	nil	1.3	30.7	nil	38.1	28.2	16.2
1979	6.8	76.7	24.2	17.9	31.9	42.8	42.4	nil	14.4	31.2
1980	7.7	79.1	25.2	19.6	41.5	31.1	100.0	nil	28.9	47.0
1981	62.6	-	33.1	17.6	23.2	27.8	47.7	30.3	30.3	46.9
1982	44.2	-	35.7	3.3	11.5	39.3	3.7	nil	27.4	36.8
1983	20.8	-	19.9	10.1	-	43.1	9.2	8.8	28.7	20.1
Benelux 1978	10.1	15.6	15.8	0.3	1.8	72.8	3.3	nil	51.2	17.1
1979	9.3	12.5	18.3	0.7	-	68.8	23.1	nil	20.2	15.7
1980	10.5	24.3	28.3	19.1	29.4	68.5	23.4	25.1	44.8	27.1
1981	53.2	-	42.1	7.6	32.8	74.5	19.5	51.3	51.3	40.4
1982	36.4	-	35.3	8.1	40.4	79.3	20.0	8.6	48.1	32.8
1983	32.8	-	30.7	11.7	-	80.7	19.6	10.5	44.7	30.2
United Kingdom 1978	21.2	34.7	31.8	16.5	48.3	92.8	28.0	11.1	38.7	30.1
1979	17.2	44.8	33.4	20.7	82.1	90.3	53.6	56.2	30.0	33.3
1980	33.5	37.7	31.3	16.2	52.0	89.5	64.8	22.9	35.0	32.1
1981	26.4	-	35.7	9.7	33.6	98.6	46.1	39.7	39.7	27.8
1982	34.9	-	32.0	13.5	44.6	99.2	42.3	17.6	42.2	31.1
1983	31.6	-	28.8	16.6	-	99.2	34.4	10.4	39.9	29.0
Ireland 1978	15.6	11.7	28.7	7.7	10.7	56.7	35.9	nil	23.7	19.6
1979	12.4	13.2	37.8	9.4	9.0	100.0	40.1	nil	23.2	22.1
1980	12.3	25.1	33.3	8.5	15.1	39.6	45.0	2.1	20.0	24.0

TABLE 3.2—Continued

Year	Sensitive industrial products (except textiles)	Semi-sensitive industrial products (except textiles)[c]	Non-sensitive industrial products (except textiles)	Sensitive textiles	Semi-sensitive textiles[d]	Non-sensitive textiles	Sensitive agricultural products[e]	Semi-sensitive agricultural products[f]	Non-sensitive agricultural products	Total agricultural and manufactured products
Ireland—cont.										
1981	19.1	-	58.2	10.9	25.2	100.0	34.3	98.1	98.1	33.3
1982	19.8	-	56.0	10.1	16.7	100.0	39.0	3.0	88.0	33.7
1983	25.8	-	34.8	8.7	-	43.5	38.6	nil	82.2	25.8
Denmark										
1978	29.2	34.4	69.3	26.1	67.8	79.5	67.0	75.3	80.9	45.1
1979	24.6	48.9	58.6	16.6	71.7	78.7	61.1	65.8	14.5	33.1
1980	29.4	47.0	60.0	10.0	47.7	98.0	63.1	55.9	48.6	37.2
1981	43.9	-	61.8	8.7	31.9	95.6	47.6	38.5	38.5	35.5
1982	40.0	-	43.8	9.0	34.8	91.6	19.6	14.7	42.0	32.9
1983	37.4	-	53.6	13.1	-	97.0	23.5	21.6	44.7	37.4
Greece										
1981	0.8	-	1.7	0.5	0.1	13.4	5.1	nil	1.4	1.7
1982	5.1	-	8.2	4.4	3.5	13.8	3.0	nil	3.3	6.2
1983	8.3	-	10.8	2.5	-	24.7	5.8	8.1	14.5	8.3

SOURCE: Microfiche data provided by the Statistical Office of the European Communities.

[a] GSP-receiving imports = all imports in GSP items which actually receive preferential treatment.
[b] GSP-covered imports = all products included in the GSP scheme.
[c] Abandoned in 1981. [d] Abandoned in 1983.

between countries. The weight which is given to tariff preferences in the investment decision finds its parallel in the relevance of export-processing zones or, more generally, free zones, in developing countries offering tax holidays.[21] The considerable differences in the success of free zones within the developing world underlines the point that tax holidays are only a complement to other macro- and micro-economic factors available in successful host countries and are ineffective without them.

The origin rules in the United States and the Community GSP schemes, however, particularly the share of domestic value-added content set by both schemes and which imports have to meet, disqualify many offshore assembly activities for GSP treatment. Additionally, any export-oriented investments in developing countries which may be stimulated by the GSP will require stable export market access conditions during the pay-off period. The discretionary elements in the United States and Community schemes which concede preferences for each product unilaterally only on a year-by-year basis, introduce a damaging degree of uncertainty. Thus GSP treatment on the present basis seems unlikely to be an adequate inducement for stimulating investment in developing beneficiary countries.

NOTES AND REFERENCES

1. For a survey of methods and results, see Baldwin, 'Trade Policies in Developed Countries', in Ronald W. Jones and Peter B. Kenen (eds), *Handbook of International Economics* (Amsterdam: North-Holland, 1984), Volume 1, pp. 572-619.

2. See EFTA, *The Trade Effects of EFTA and the EEC 1959-67* (Geneva, 1972) and Ann Weston *et al.*, *The EEC's Generalised System of Preferences* (London: Overseas Development Institute, 1980).

3. A somewhat cruder method consists of replacing the tariff variable by a dummy variable reflecting the GSP status of a country.

4. See André Sapir, 'Trade Benefits Under the EEC Generalized System of Preferences', *European Economic Review* 15, June 1981, No. 3, pp. 339-355.

5. See Baldwin and Murray, 'MFN Tariff Reductions and Developing Country Trade Benefits Under the GSP' *Economic Journal* 87, March 1977, pp. 30-46. The paper makes a diagrammatic presentation of the *ex-ante* method.

6. See Sapir and Lars Lundberg, 'The US Generalised System of Preferences and its Impacts', in Baldwin and Krueger (eds), *op. cit.*, pp. 195-231.

7. US International Trade Commission, *An Evaluation of US Imports under the Generalized System of Preferences*. USITC Publication 1379 (Washington: 1983).

8. Sapir and Lundberg, *op. cit.*

9. See Baldwin and Murray, *op. cit.*, and Thomas Bayard and M. Moore, *Trade and Employment Effects of the US Generalized System of Preferences*. Office of Foreign Economic Research, US Department of Labor (Washington: 1979), mimeographed.

10. For details, see Sapir and Lundberg, *op. cit.*, Tables 4 and A.1.

11. For details, see Sapir and Lundberg, *op. cit.*, Tables 5 and A.2.

12. Baldwin and Murray, *op. cit.*

13. See Murray, *op. cit.*, pp. 64-71, and Michael Rom, *The Role of Tariff Quotas in Commercial Policy*, (London: Macmillan for Trade Policy Research Centre, 1979), Part III.

14. Canada, which established its scheme by mid-1974, is included because of data constraints. Since the Canadian share in the total imports of both countries is low, the distortion effect should be low as well.

15. For further details on the results presented in this section, see Rolf J. Langhammer, *Ten Years of the EEC's Generalized System of Preferences for Developing Countries: Success or Failure?*, Kiel Working Paper, No. 183, September 1983.

16. Sapir, *op. cit.*

17. Baldwin and Murray, *op. cit.*

18. In 1973 the average import value-weighted GSP preference margins in the Community amounted to 10.1 percentage points. See Axel Borrmann, Christine Borrmann, Manfred Stegger, *Das Allgemeine Zollpräferenzsystem der EG* (Hamburg: Weltarchiv, 1979), p. 125.

19. Langhammer, *op. cit.*

20. The following cross-product equation has been estimated:

$$\log_0 n \left(\frac{q_{is}^1}{q_{is}^0} \Big/ \frac{q_{js}^1}{q_{js}^0} \right) = a_1 + a \log_0 n \left(\frac{P_{is}^1}{P_{is}^0} \Big/ \frac{P_{js}^1}{P_{js}^0} \right) + e$$

where q_{is} and q_{js} are the quantities of Community imports from all GSP beneficiaries i (less developed countries including Yugoslavia and excluding Taiwan) and all non-beneficiaries j (developed and centrally planned economies excluding Yugoslavia and including Taiwan) in the non-sensitive manufactured product s, and P_{is} and P_{js} are the unit values respectively. The indices 1 and 0 denote the years 1972 and 1970. The estimate based on 36 non-sensitive items exceeding a value of imports from GSP beneficiaries of EUA2 million in 1980, yielded the following regression coefficients (t-values in paranthesis):

a_0	a_1	R^2
- 0.48	- 1.10	0.42
(3.62)	(4.99)	

21. Export processing zones or free zones allow goods to be moved into the zone without payment of customs duties. Firms processing goods for export in such zones are often exempted from labour market legislation prevailing in the rest of the country (for example, minimum wages) and enjoy further tax holidays.

Chapter 4

Distribution of Benefits from GSP Schemes

IN THIS chapter an attempt is made to answer the following questions: (i) who are the major beneficiaries of the GSP among the exporting countries and (ii) who are the major beneficiaries as between the exporters in the beneficiary countries and importers in the donor countries

In general, the benefits of the GSP will accrue not only to consumers in the importing countries, but also to the importers and the exporters. No benefit to consumers will occur, however, if the importers or exporters keep the preference margins for themselves. This can happen if importers keep their prices to consumers unchanged after the introduction of preferences or if exporters raise their prices to the importers by the amount of the preference margin. In the former case, the income gain accrues to importers and in the latter case, to exporters. It is, however, more likely that the gains will be shared among consumers who benefit from lower prices, exporters (who raise the export price by part of the tariff reduction), and importers (who benefit from lower prices brought about by the tariff reduction but do not pass on the whole price reduction to consumers). The exact distribution of income gains depends on the degree of competition in the market, on the supply and demand elasticities and on the relative bargaining power of the exporters versus importers.

THE AMERICAN SCHEME

For beneficiary developing countries to expand their exports (and market shares) to the United States in response to the GSP, they are dependent, in the first place, upon the amount of their trade which is subject to MFN duties. According to this criterion, the main beneficiary exporters in 1979 were Taiwan, Mexico, the Republic of Korea, Hong Kong and Brazil; see Table 4.1, column 2. Apart from the amount of dutiable trade, the commodity structure and the GSP product coverage of each beneficiary determine the extent of its GSP-eligible trade. Among the countries included in Table 4.1, these two factors have been relatively favourable for Chile, the Dominican Republic and Haiti all of which have a high ratio of GSP-eligible trade to MFN-dutiable trade. For Malaysia, the Philippines, the Republic of Korea and India, however, the ratio of GSP-eligible trade to MFN-dutiable trade is under 30 per cent.

As well as the level of eligible trade, the potential effect of the GSP also depends upon the size of the preference margin. This margin is potentially equal to the MFN duty on eligible products, of which the weighted average is shown in Table 4.1, column 4. As has been shown, however, because of various exclusions, beneficiary countries, in practice, continue to pay MFN duties on some GSP-eligible products. The weighted average of the duty on these products appears in column 5 of Table 4.1.

The difference between the MFN and GSP duties is the actual preference margin which, as the figures in column 6 indicate, varies substantially across beneficiaries. The figures in column 7 show in each case the percentage of GSP-eligible imports that actually entered the United States free of duty. To obtain the value of GSP duty-free imports, columns 3 and 7 are multiplied together (not shown in Table 4.1). The top five countries here are (by decreasing order of importance): Taiwan, the Republic of Korea, Brazil, Hong Kong and Mexico. Together, these countries accounted in 1979 for about 70 per cent of the GSP duty-free imports of the United States.

TABLE 4.1

US Imports, Duties and Preference Margins for Beneficiary Countries with over $100 million of GSP-eligible Imports, 1979

| Country | Imports ($US millions) | | | Duties and preference on eligible trade (per cent) | | | | Ranking | | Actual preference margin on total dutiable trade (%)[a] | Tariff revenue foregone ($ millions) |
	Total (1)	MFN dutiable (2)	GSP eligible (3)	MFN duty[a] (4)	GSP duty[a] (5)	Actual reference margin[a] (6)	Ratio between actual and theoretical preference margins[b] (7)	MFN duty (8)	Actual reference margin (9)	(10)	(11)
Mexico	8,980	5,491	1,927	7.50	5.12	2.37	32	7	15	0.83	45
Taiwan	6,426	6,305	2,526	9.22	2.87	6.35	69	3	4	2.54	160
Korea	4,348	3,907	1,151	9.23	2.46	6.77	73	2	2	1.99	78

Hong Kong	4,289	3,566	1,611	10.00	6.06	3.94	39	1	10	1.78	63
Brazil	3,383	1,852	947	3.74	0.89	2.84	76	17	13	1.45	27
Malaysia	2,249	923	184	4.97	3.19	1.78	36	16	17	0.35	3
Philippines	1,648	1,238	305	6.70	2.91	3.79	57	13	11	0.93	12
Singapore	1,532	1,197	372	7.63	2.85	4.77	63	6	8	1.48	18
Peru	1,235	381	187	5.29	1.90	3.39	64	15	12	1.66	6
India	1,148	672	184	6.74	1.43	5.32	80	12	7	1.46	24
Israel	774	652	299	8.34	0.34	7.99	96	5	1	3.66	24
Dominican R.	720	329	210	6.66	5.74	0.93	14	14	18	0.59	2
Thailand	646	299	111	7.38	1.91	5.47	74	8	5	2.03	6
Argentina	634	404	177	6.98	2.94	4.04	58	10	9	1.77	7
Chile	468	251	233	3.03	1.08	1.95	64	18	16	1.81	5
Yugoslavia	406	353	179	7.28	0.75	6.53	90	9	3	3.31	12
Portugal	272	259	116	6.88	1.41	5.40	78	11	6	2.42	6
Haiti	234	177	100	8.62	6.14	2.48	29	4	14	1.40	2
All beneficiaries	51,170	38,164	11,725	7.98	3.48	4.50	56	-	-	1.38	528

SOURCE: Data provided by the Office of the US Trade Representative.
[a] The figures in columns 4, 5, 6 and 10 are weighted average tariff rates.
[b] Column 6 divided by column 4.

Obviously, the level of GSP covered imports can be a very misleading indicator of trade benefits. What is really needed is an estimate of the additional trade afforded by the GSP. It is possible to obtain estimates of the trade effects (trade creation only) for individual beneficiaries. The results indicate a very high concentration of the trade creation effect in favour of Hong Kong, the Republic of Korea and Taiwan which account for two thirds of the total effect. Moreover, the top 10 countries share 90 per cent of the trade effect.

As far as the distribution of benefits between exporting and importing countries is concerned, the tariff revenue foregone by the United States on GSP trade is shown in Table 4.1. The figures were obtained by multiplying the *actual* preference margin by the value of GSP-eligible trade. If markets for imported goods were competitive, the tariff revenue foregone would indicate the maximum increase in export earnings by beneficiary countries as a result of the GSP. In reality, however, part of this potential benefit will be captured by powerful American importers or intermediate traders.[1]

THE EUROPEAN COMMUNITY SCHEME

The distribution among beneficiaries of both GSP-receiving imports and MFN-dutiable imports of GSP items in 1973 and 1983 shown in Table 4.2 sheds some light on which countries have gained from the Community scheme. The ranking of the ten largest suppliers underwent considerable changes during the eight years under consideration. Whereas Yugoslavia held the top rank in 1973 (with about one third of the GSP-receiving imports into the Community), it had disappeared from the list in 1983. Instead, Brazil moved into the top place followed by a number of Asian countries. The presence of oil-exporting countries like Iran in 1973 and Romania in 1983 in the list indicates that the GSP covers some medium and heavy oils or petroleum gases (MFN tariff 1.5 per cent!) which hardly suffer from market access barriers. With these products the Community inflates its GSP offer without stimulating trade.

In general, the ranking shows that a growing number of countries, mainly from Asia, now participate in the GSP, so that the ten largest suppliers accounted for only two thirds of all GSP-receiving imports in 1983 compared to more than 86 per cent ten years ago. What seems to be more relevant is the extent to which the GSP-covered exports from each country actually received preferential treatment. In this respect the countries range between two extremes. One limit is set by a country like Venezuela which receives GSP treatment on almost all of its GSP-eligible exports. Venezuela exports only oil derivatives, has no problems with origin rules and distributes its products via GSP experienced traders.

At the other end of the scale is a country like Hong Kong, which exports many sensitive products that have strictly applied limits to duty-free access. Hong Kong also encounters problems with origin rules which disqualify many of its GSP-covered exports from preferential treatment. An example of this is the case of men's and boy's shirts of synthetic textiles fibres (BTN 6103-11) worth 182 million European Units of Account (EUA) which Hong Kong exported to the Community in 1983. Only 0.8 per cent of these exports entered the market duty-free under the GSP. This very low percentage has nothing to do with the tariff quota, since no MFN duty was re-imposed on Hong Kong exports. The reason for the exclusion was that the fabric from which the shirts were made had been imported into Hong Kong. To qualify for GSP treatment under the GSP scheme, it is necessary for the *yarn* (and not the fabric) to be imported; if it is not, then the finished product is not eligible for preferential treatment. This is because of the rules about the amount of value added in the exporting country.

To ascertain the income distribution effect of the Community GSP scheme, an estimate is needed of the amount of tariff revenues foregone (irrespective of whether this amount is pocketed by the importer or transferred to the exporting countries). Under the assumption of a zero price elasticity of demand in the relevant range and of an average preference margin of ten percentage points, the tariff revenue loss in 1981 amounted to about EUA850 million. To put this figure into perspective, it is 8.4 per cent of total Development Assistance Committee (DAC) development aid in 1981. The amount of EUA 850 million is not the relevant figure to use, however, since it is by no means guaranteed that this amount accrues

TABLE 4.2

Community Imports of GSP Products from the
Ten Largest Beneficiaries, 1973 and 1983

Beneficiaries	GSP-receiving imports[a]	MFN-dutiable imports[b]	Beneficiaries	GSP-receiving imports[a]	MFN-dutiable imports[b]
	1973			1983	
Yugoslavia	33.9	33.4	Brazil	11.5	5.1
Rep. of Korea	10.1	6.5	India	8.2	3.6
Brazil	8.5	4.8	Hong Kong	8.1	13.7
Iran	6.9	11.5	Rep. of Korea	7.5	9.3
Argentina	5.7	3.5	China	7.1	4.4
Hong Kong	5.1	11.3	Malaysia	5.6	2.2
India	4.9	3.6	Thailand	4.4	4.4
Singapore	4.1	6.3	Romania	4.3	3.9
Mexico	3.8	2.5	Singapore	4.3	4.0
Pakistan	3.8	2.7	Philippines	4.2	1.5
Total of the ten largest suppliers	86.8	86.1	Total of the ten largest suppliers	65.2	52.1

SOURCES: Axel Borrmann *et al.*, *op. cit.*; Statistical Office of the European Communities.
[a]Share of total imports actually receiving preferential treatment.
[b]Share of total imports of GSP items which did not receive preferential treatment.

to beneficiary exporters. In practice, an essential precondition of benefit accruing to the exporting country would be for the exporter to be sure that his product will enter the Community under GSP conditions. This is not the case for sensitive items, which in 1981 accounted for 50 per cent of total Community GSP-receiving imports.

An example will illustrate the point. A West German importer may order tiles — one of the very sensitive products with country-specific quotas — from the Republic of Korea. The correct formalities are completed by the Korean exporter (certificate of origin, *et cetera*) but if the tiles are shipped in the autumn, they may stay in a bonded warehouse until the beginning of the following year in order that they may qualify under the tariff quota for that year. When the tiles are declared to the customs authorities at the beginning of the year, there may be a further delay before the importer is informed whether his consignment has been admitted free of duty. (The quota for this product is usually exhausted within the first week of January). The exporter in the Republic of Korea receives no information on which of his exports to the Federal Republic of Germany entered the market duty-free. Because of this uncertainty, the importer will price the goods under MFN conditions and will look upon any preferences received as a windfall to be used, perhaps, for subsidizing further sales by special offers or discounts to the retail trade.

There is thus no chance for the exporter of sensitive products to anticipate preferential treatment and thus to raise his export prices in advance by the amount of the preference margins. Even if tariff quotas are pre-allocated to traditional importers so that there is no uncertainty, the exporter may not benefit because there are numerous sources of low-priced sensitive goods and thus, intense competition in the markets for those goods. Typically, buyers' market conditions prevail which means that importers can rapidly replace one supplier with another.

For non-sensitive and non-standardized products with open-ended ceilings the preconditions for an 'aid' transfer are certainly better, unless the independent price bargaining between importers and exporters is conditioned by transfer pricing. This could occur in intra-firm trade such as in the Volkswagen case where intermediate products are exported to the parent company under GSP conditions.

On the assumption that the preference margin amounts to ten percentage points and that the tariff revenues foregone are fully distributed to the individual GSP beneficiaries, the aid transfer element in the Community GSP shrinks to a negligible quantity if non-sensitive products only are taken into account. In these conditions the aid transfer accruing to all exporters of non-sensitive GSP items, would have amounted to about EUA420 million in 1981, which equals 4.2 per cent of total DAC development aid in 1981.

The mirror of 'benefit' sharing among beneficiaries is what is often referred to as 'burden' sharing among Community member states. They are concerned about job losses caused by improved market access for the exports of developing countries. It may be argued that, without large benefits, there is little 'burden' to be shared. This global macroeconomic view, however, has been widely challenged by the sectorally confined view of politicians who are concerned about job losses in vulnerable industries and who wish each member state to take an 'equal' share in assuming this 'burden'. For that reason the Community has determined the global 'absorptive capacity' of each member by such crude criteria as population, Gross National Product (GNP) and size of foreign trade. The shares of member states based on these criteria are, with few exceptions, the same for all products.[2]

In practice, however, there appears to be no conformity between the arbitrarily fixed shares and the actual distribution. Throughout the period 1978-83 French imports fell short of their share whereas West Germany, the United Kingdom and Italy in some cases exceeded their shares. Not too much should be made of this distribution, therefore, although different national interests and protectionist attitudes may have an influence on it. Thus, member states like France are evidently in favour of a more restrictive way of applying preferences in the face of strong pressures from domestic entrepreneurs and some ACP exporters. The United Kingdom, on the other hand, has tried to continue its historical world market orientation in agricultural products.

If actual duty-free imports are adjusted for differences in the domestic market size of the members (as measured by their income) it turns out that in 1981 West Germany, as well as the United Kingdom and the Benelux countries, imported twice as much as France in sensitive products, including textiles. A similar difference between France and the other Community members emerges if population, instead of income is taken as the measure of market size. This accords with what has been observed of Community internal negotiations on the annual GSP concession schedules. The French delegates usually emerge as the main proponents of further restrictions to the scheme. In this respect, however, the 'imitation' effect, as well as the political tensions which arise from the discrepancies between major and minor 'bearers of burden' within the Community, give more cause for concern than the protectionist attitudes of a single member country.

DISTRIBUTION OF BENEFITS COMPARED

When the ranking of major beneficiaries under the two GSP schemes is compared, the common pattern emerges of the top places being taken by the newly industrializing countries like the Republic of Korea, Brazil and Hong Kong. There are, however, two major differences, between the United States and the Community. First, Taiwan is excluded from the Community scheme, whereas it is the leading beneficiary in the American scheme. In spite of its exclusion, however, Taiwan also performed extraordinarily well in the Community market and its record bears comparison with the three other 'Gang of Four' members (the Republic of Korea, Singapore and Hong Kong) which receive preferences.

Second, in the Community ranking, oil-exporting countries like Romania, Venezuela and Saudi Arabia keep high positions because of oil derivatives exported under the GSP. These countries do not appear in the American ranking because OPEC members are excluded from the American scheme. What is also clear is that the smaller and poorer countries have not benefitted to any extent from either the American or the

Community schemes.

An important difference between the two schemes shows up when consideration is given to whether the importer or the exporter obtains the benefits in terms of tariff revenue foregone. In general, the United States scheme is more transparent and hence less uncertain because of its more open-ended character. The Community scheme, with its numerous limitations, involves a great deal of uncertainty for the exporters and thus enables importers to appropriate tariff revenues foregone. The chances for exporters to raise prices by the amount of preference margins and thus to increase their profit margins, however, are better in the American scheme only at first glance. Discretionary elements such as the loss of preferential treatment once certain export amounts have been exceeded in the previous year, have essentially the same uncertainty effects on exporters as in the Community scheme.

Hence, in both schemes the distribution of benefits tends to favour the importers. This is explicitly the case for the Community scheme in the short run because of the 'greyhound' system of allocating tariff quotas to importers (first come, first served). Implicitly in the medium term, however, this also holds for the American scheme because individual exporters in developing countries do not know in the first part of the year whether their product has reached the limits of the competitive-need clause in the previous year and will thus be excluded from beneficiary status. The short-term discretionary decisions of the donor countries tend to enable importers rather than exporters to benefit from the preferential duty. Regardless of this distribution, however, the absolute amount of this sort of 'aid' would still remain negligible compared to official aid even if it could be fully shifted to the exporters. The next chapter will look more closely at the administrative rules governing the two schemes.

NOTES AND REFERENCES

1. This point is made by Rachel McCulloch and Jose Pinera, 'Trade as Aid: The Political Economy of Tariff Preferences for

Developing Countries.' *American Economic Review* 67, 1977, December, pp. 959-67.

2. In 1980, the actual distribution of 80 per cent of the global tariff quota for each product was as follows (in per cent): Benelux 10.5, Denmark 5, West Germany 27.5, Greece 2, France 19, Ireland 0.5, Italy 14.5, and United Kingdom 21. The share for plywood and veneer and five other sensitive agricultural products are different in order to take account of the United Kingdom's traditional imports from the two ASEAN Commonwealth members, Malaysia and Singapore. A so-called Community reserve (20 per cent of the global tariff quota) to be allocated to Community countries which have already exhausted their shares and are prepared to import more on a duty-free basis, should allow for more flexibility. However, much more flexibility is provided by the indirect imports and the duty-free circulation within the Community once a product has entered the market than by this bureaucratic procedure.

Chapter 5

GSP Administrative Rules and their Trade Effects

IN CHAPTER 2, it was shown that both the Community and American schemes are subject to a number of administrative rules that limit the preferential treatment received by developing countries. In this chapter the actual importance of those rules is examined and the effects on trade are assessed.

RULES AND LIMITATIONS OF THE AMERICAN SCHEME

A rough idea of the importance of the various exclusions presently built into the American GSP scheme can be obtained by examining the trade flows presented in Table 3.1. For instance, in 1978, American imports from developing countries amounted to $US75.9 billion. Out of this sum, $US62.0 billion were subject to MFN tariffs and thus constitute the potential trade that could benefit from GSP treatment. However, because of restrictive country coverage, only $US31.4 billion of dutiable imports from developing nations came from GSP beneficiaries.[1] Moreover, within this amount, only $US9.7 billion was eligible for GSP treatment because of product exclusions, most of which covered items with relatively high MFN tariff rates. Finally, the implementation of rules of origin and competitive-need limitations further reduced the actual GSP duty-free imports to $US5.2 billion.

Further information on the effect of administrative rules can be gleaned by examining the proportion of GSP-eligible exports from individual beneficiary countries that actually received GSP treatment (Table 4.1). This proportion is directly related to the application of rules of origin and competitive-need limitations. In general, it is to be expected that rules of origin will affect mainly small and specialized countries exporting highly processed goods with a high ratio of imported intermediate goods to sales value. It should be noted, however, that a major share of the trade which is denied GSP treatment because of the application of rules of origin, enters the United States under offshore assembly reduced-duty treatment. Competitive-need limitations, on the other hand, should mainly affect large and/or highly specialized countries.

The figures in column 7 of Table 4.1 indicate that the countries most adversely affected by the administrative rules are the Dominican Republic, Haiti, and Mexico, while those least affected are Israel, Yugoslavia, and India. The actual margin of preference was the highest for Israel, the Republic of Korea, and Yugoslavia, and the lowest for the Dominican Republic, Malaysia, and Chile (column 9 of Table 4.1). Although it is difficult to specify the reasons for these rather surprising findings within the scope of this essay, the different product composition of exports from the individual countries obviously account for the major part of them.

It is sometimes argued that competitive-need limitations should, in principle, favour both American producers and low-income developing countries at the expense of large and established exporters in developing countries. Whether these limitations benefit the poorest developing countries, however, merits further examination.

One measure of the impact of competitive-need limitations on beneficiary countries is the ratio between the actual and theoretical preference margins which is given in column 7 of Table 4.1. A system of limitations that benefits the poorest countries would imply a negative correlation between this ratio and an index of the level of development like *per capita* GNP. Although such an index is not shown in Table 4.1 nevertheless it is clear that the poorer countries do not appear to be gaining much advantage from the scheme. It would thus seem that the main effect of competitive-need limitations has been to protect American producers rather than to redistribute the benefits of the GSP to the least developed countries.

For Hong Kong, the Republic of Korea and Taiwan, the top three beneficiaries identified in Chapter 4 as accounting for two-thirds of the total GSP effect, the average ratio of the actual preference margin to the theoretical preference margin is 60 per cent but with a ratio of 39 per cent for Hong Kong and 73 per cent for the Republic of Korea. If the ratios for the other beneficiary countries are averaged, then the figure is also about 60 per cent, but the variation is, if anything, greater with Haiti at 29 per cent and Israel at 96 per cent. On this comparison, it would appear that the administrative rules were uneven in their effects discriminating against some large exporters in terms of value of exports (Mexico and Hong Kong) and not others (Taiwan and the Republic of Korea). Countries which seem to have gained most from the GSP scheme (Israel and Yugoslavia) do not appear to have been affected by either rules of origin or competitive-need limitations.

Administrative rules, by introducing uncertainties in the functioning of the system have probably restricted the growth of exports from beneficiaries. Indeed, the way the competitive-need limitations are operated makes it difficult to assess whether or when a particular supplying country will lose its beneficiary status for a given product. For instance, during the period January 1976 to March 1983, India lost the benefit of GSP status on 42 products. The average period without preferences was three years, not necessarily consecutive, but only three products were excluded from GSP treatment for the entire period.

Since March 1981, a system of 'discretionary graduation' has added a new source of uncertainty to the United States scheme. Under this additional limitation, every year the American Administration permanently excludes specific products exported by certain countries from GSP eligibility in response to petitions filed by American producers or labour unions. Decisions to remove these products from the list of

GSP-eligible items are based on a country's level of development, its competitiveness in the particular product and the overall economic interests of the United States. So far, the top seven beneficiaries — Taiwan, the Republic of Korea, Hong Kong, Mexico, Brazil, Singapore and Israel — have, to varying degrees, been affected by discretionary graduation. These countries were already affected by competitive-need limitations in respect of many products. Some American importers have been complaining about the fact that the rules governing discretionary graduation are too vague and give rise to arbitrary decisions by the Administration.

EUROPEAN COMMUNITY SCHEME RULES

Administrative rules, which cover the monitoring and control of tariff quotas, ceilings, *butoirs*, origin rules and direct shipping certificates are the most crucial barriers to the effectiveness of the Community GSP scheme. The rules reflect the underlying philosophy of the scheme which is that exporting countries which are successful must be restricted in order to guarantee other beneficiaries a piece of the cake. Administrative rules are designed to direct trade which is subject to GSP treatment according to politically determined criteria such as an 'equal distribution of benefits' and the 'burden sharing principle'. Trading under such a system of preferences, with 'closed' quotas newly determined each calendar year, is like a game of hazard which has its heyday in the greyhound race in January each year and then slows down until the beginning of the next year. Production and transport services in developing countries may adjust to this rhythm by, for instance, closing producing plants in certain months each year in order to minimize the storage and transportation costs of sensitive items.

The rate at which tariff quotas for sensitive items is exhausted is shown in Table 5.1. The table is for imports into West Germany but the experience of other countries will not be very different. In 1982, for example, within the first month of the year Brazil had used up most of its quota for *general* textile imports into West Germany. This does not mean that the quota on each *individual* textile commodity had been exhausted — indeed, 1.4 per cent of the total quota was still unused at the end of the year — but that overall, the quota was nearly fully utilized in the first month. (See Table 5.1.) For most textile products from Brazil into West Germany, therefore, the MFN tariff was re-imposed in less than one month. Similarly, country-specific tariff quotas in industrial products (excluding textiles) were almost completely exhausted by the seven largest exporting countries in the course of 1982. The lowest rate of utilization for all products excluding textiles in the West German market was in India at 83.2 in 1982. Utilization rates in textiles were generally lower and fluctuated widely between countries, but this seems to be the consequence mainly of the restrictive origin rules.

In addition to the restriction of preferences for successful exporting countries and the separation of the Community into its individual member countries for the purpose of granting preference quotas, the Community scheme has a further element of uncertainty and unattractiveness for beneficiaries. This is that the administrative rules are published so late each year that the exporting countries cannot adjust to any changes which are made for the ensuing year. Indeed, it is sometimes not even possible to know the exact GSP status and rules for an individual product one week before the new rules come into operation in any one year. For instance, preferences for 1982, were approved by the Council of Ministers on 7 December 1981, and were published in detail in the Official Journal of the Community of 21 December 1981. This issue of the journal was not generally available until 30 December 1981, five days before the new set of tariff quotas for 1982 were to come into force. The same thing happened in 1983. Though draft schedules of the tariff quotas are available earlier, they are recommendations only and cannot be regarded as final decisions, since the Council often changes details within the different product categories. It is, of course, essential for individual exporters to be aware of the detailed provisions.[2]

TABLE 5.1

Utilization Rate of Tariff Quotas for Sensitive GSP Items on the West German Market 1977 and 1982, by Major Beneficiaries

| Beneficiary | | Utilization rate[a] | | Percentage share of products in imports of sensitive items receiving GSP treatment on which MFN tariff was re-imposed within: | | | | | | | |
| | | | | First month | | First quarter | | First half | | Full year | |
		All products[b]	Textiles	All products[b]	Textiles	All products[b]	Textiles	All products[b]	Textiles	All products[b]	Textiles
Brazil	1977	9.7	17.4	11.4	16.3	23.6	41.4	23.8	43.4	79.1	96.2
	1982	96.6	98.6	18.3	94.7	46.1	97.7	46.1	97.9	54.8	97.9
Hong Kong	1977	25.6	61.5	49.4	nil	78.1	37.5	87.0	37.5	87.0	37.5
	1982	99.6	82.1	40.1	35.9	84.5	62.8	84.5	67.7	95.7	91.5
India	1977	2.9	25.0	4.8	41.4	4.8	97.2	39.5	97.3	39.5	97.3
	1982	83.2	75.0	nil	18.9	nil	77.8	nil	77.8	nil	88.7
Singapore	1977	0.9	8.6	18.2	15.9	18.2	100.0	18.2	100.0	18.2	100.0
	1982	97.4	68.0	nil	9.0	nil	55.9	nil	55.9	99.7	73.3
South Korea	1977	41.6	18.8	50.9	43.2	82.2	81.9	82.2	83.3	82.2	96.5
	1982	97.1	99.5	27.1	37.2	65.3	86.9	73.7	94.0	95.9	99.9
Thailand	1977	5.0	14.0	1.6	85.5	1.6	99.7	1.6	99.7	1.6	100.0
	1982	nil	89.3	nil	18.8	nil	54.3	nil	64.1	nil	89.1
Yugoslavia	1977	30.1	11.0	9.5	6.8	91.7	9.5	93.4	9.5	93.4	23.6
	1982	100.0	nil	40.5	nil	100.0	nil	100.0	nil	100.0	nil

SOURCE: Federal Ministry of Economics, Bonn.
[a]Percentage share of GSP-receiving imports in tariff quotas guaranteed for individual beneficiaries
[b]Excluding textiles.

65

The tardy publication of the annual quotas and rules governing the preference scheme combined with the rigid upper limits to the preference concessions make the Community scheme of doubtful benefit to exporting countries. Exporters and importers, who make their decisions six months or so before tariff quotas and rules are fixed by the Community, will therefore be making their decisions (particularly in the case of products which are on the border line of tariff preference) in conditions of uncertainty. They are likely, therefore, to set their prices on the assumption that tariffs will be payable. Under such conditions any significant trade expansion effect from the preference schemes seems highly unlikely.

COMPARISON OF ADMINISTRATIVE RULES

As has been shown, administrative rules do not play the same role in the Community and American schemes. In the Community, where the product coverage of the GSP is extensive, administrative rules represent the major limitation on the effectiveness of the scheme. Such rules are a less important limitation in the American case where important product categories are excluded outright from preferential treatment.

Administrative rules dealing with tariff quotas introduce uncertainty into the Community scheme. This is because tariff quotas are a key aspect of the arrangements. Given such a system, it is often impossible for an exporter to know whether a particular shipment to the Community will benefit from GSP treatment. The effect of this uncertainty, as shown in Chapter 4, is that exporters may not be willing, for fear of losing their markets, to adjust their prices in anticipation of their goods being imported duty-free. The benefit of any preferential duty which is then granted will accrue to the importers (and possibly the consumers) in the country and not to the exporters in the developing countries. There is little or no evidence to indicate that the complicated administrative rules of the Community scheme which are designed to ensure a 'share of the cake' for the least developed countries, are proving effective.

There is no uncertainty within each 12 month period for exporters to the United States. As from the end of March each year, exporters will know precisely which of their products will qualify for GSP treatment and their shipments can be made accordingly. The uncertainty in the American scheme is whether the same products will qualify for GSP treatment in succeeding years. The competitive-need rule may be brought into effect (see Chapter 4) so that an exporter of a particular product which has sold well in the American market in one year may find this product excluded in the following year. This rule has the intention and the effect of protecting domestic producers to the detriment of exporters in developing countries.

TRADE EFFECTS OF THE GSP

To conclude this chapter, an assessment is made of the effects at the administrative rules on trade creation and trade diversion. Because of the differences in implementation of the schemes in the Community and the United States, each scheme is assessed separately.

As was shown in Chapter 3, the empirical estimates which have been made of trade diversion and trade creation in the Community are somewhat inconclusive. One of the reasons for this appears to be the mass of tariff quotas, ceilings, origin rules and the 'each product, each year' administration of preferences. Taken together, they introduce much uncertainty and give rise to windfall gains for importers. Hence, the trade effects are relatively small compared to the potential gains from a system of generalized preferences unhampered by restrictions.

It was pointed out in Chapter 3 that the opportunities for trade diversion under the Community scheme are limited because only a few countries receive less favourable tariff treatment than the developing countries. Quotas, as well as other restrictions on 'sensitive' products, also limit the scope for trade creation.

The American scheme, on the other hand has probably resulted in more trade effects than the Community scheme partly because of a more transparent system of administration and the absence of free trade arrangements with major trading partners. The estimates presented in Chapter 3 suggest that trade creation is about two-and-half times larger than trade diversion.

In the next chapter, the effectiveness of the two schemes will be considered in a broader context.

NOTES AND REFERENCES

1. Of the $US30.6 billion excluded because of country restrictions, over 90 per cent came from OPEC countries. Since the MFN duty on oil is very low, the loss of preferences from these restrictions is not very important.

2. The changes may affect either the GSP status of a product (for example titanium oxides [BTN 28.25]. This was recommended by the Commission as a non-sensitive product for 1982, but was changed into a sensitive product by the Council). Alternatively, the amount of tariff quotas could be amended, (for example, in leather clothing [BTN 42.03], the Council cut the tariff quotas recommended by the Commission by 5 per cent and included China, Hong Kong and Romania in the list of very competitive beneficiaries, in addition to the Republic of Korea which was the only country the Commission proposed). In general, the Council tends to change the recommendations of the Commission in a restrictive direction.

Chapter 6

Review of the GSP and its Future Prospects

AFTER MORE than a decade of operation, there is not much evidence of the effectiveness of the GSP. Newly emerging exporting countries in the developing world have not been able to benefit much from the GSP, which is more restrictive than special preferences, such as those contained in the Lomé Convention. The more advanced exporting countries have, in general, performed extremely well in spite of GSP restrictions, even including those denied GSP preferences altogether (for example, Taiwan in the Community market). For the 'exporters of the second generation', that is, those countries which are trying to diversify their exports, it is uncertain whether and to what extent the GSP has proved to be helpful. It should therefore be asked what would have happened if the developing countries had invested their efforts in securing further MFN tariff reductions instead of the GSP schemes.

It is true that preferences can be beneficial in the short run if they are granted to those goods where developing countries have both an intrinsic comparative advantage and superior international competitiveness in practice. It is also true that income transfers to developing countries will take place as a result of GSP Schemes if preferences are guaranteed and open-ended and they concentrate on those goods where the relative bargaining power of the beneficiaries is strong *vis-à-vis* the donor countries. But what was the probability, at the end of the 1960s, that developed countries would concentrate their concessions on such goods? For various reasons, this did not happen.

First, the GSP was sponsored by the Group of 77 and by accepting this initiative, the developed countries were able to divert attention from other mechanisms of international redistribution of income, such as the link between aid and special drawing rights, more official aid, commodity price agreements, *et cetera*. The GSP proved to be a good area for compromise with the Group of 77 without, in practice, the developed countries having to give too much away.

Second, the developing countries focussed their requests for GSP on manufactures and semi-manufactures instead of on processed agricultural products for which, given their resource endowments, many of them had more promising export opportunities. Concessions were granted in the 1970s on some processed agricultural products, but only because of the refusal of the donors to give larger concessions for industrial goods of interest to developing countries.

Third, apart from the fact that the GSP was a gift which the Group of 77 had no choice but to accept, developing countries did not expect that the individual developed countries would each produce very different schemes reflecting their different internal interests and pressures as well as their regional affiliations (Community/Africa; United States/Latin America; Japan/Southeast Asia). Market separation through minutely defined origin rules, exceptions and limitations — again different for each donor — was the consequence of such policies. Thus, a product having a domestic value added content of x per cent could be exported under the GSP to donor A, but not to donor B. Different techniques for exports to different markets would have been necessary in order to conform to the market separation, which emerged under the GSP scheme. Finally, the GSP schemes do not give any long-term — or even medium term-stability. Preferential treatment is conceded 'each year for each product' and thus is unlikely to attract foreign investment because of the uncertainty of market access. The Group of 77, in seeking a better product coverage, appear to have under-estimated the importance to export-oriented multinational companies of free access to developed-country markets.

Objectives of the GSP

In order to consider more fully whether the objectives of the GSP schemes have been achieved, it is necessary to reconsider the reason for their introduction. It was agreed, initially, that the GSP should be generalized, non-discriminatory and non-reciprocal. It was introduced in the expectation that its operation would lead to increased export earnings in developing countries, which would promote their industrialization and accelerate their rate of economic growth.

Both the Community and the American schemes give rise to serious doubts about their adequacy in achieving the original objectives of the GSP. First, the country coverage is arbitrarily fixed by the donors and each donor uses different criteria to select beneficiaries. Thus, Taiwan is excluded in the Community scheme but included in the American scheme. Second, by fixing country-specific and product-specific limits, either by competitive-need clauses or by tariff quotas and ceilings, discrimination between beneficiaries is introduced. The Community has moved in this direction very extensively — in line with its overall trade policy — but the United States also applies discriminatory rules. Third, preferences are by no means non-reciprocal. They are not negotiable, but the two major donors link their concessions to their perceptions of conduct on the part of the beneficiaries. Thus, the Community does not give GSP concessions to MFA products if a developing country refuses to sign a voluntary export restraint agreement. The United States denies preferences to countries which do not follow the American perception on how to treat foreign investments, how to deal with trade in narcotics, and how to trade in oil.

Doubts may also be expressed as to whether the GSP has to any degree stimulated export earnings and the economic growth of individual beneficiaries. Incremental trade resulting from the GSP has been found to be rather low and, because of the restrictive limitations in the schemes, duty-free exports have remained far below the amount of potential GSP-eligible exports. The uncertainty element which is inherent in the schemes has made it difficult, if not impossible, to raise export prices in the expectation of preferential treatment.

Last but not least, economic growth could have been enhanced if there had been a bigger inflow of export-oriented foreign investments from donor countries to the beneficiaries. It appears, however, that the GSP can stimulate foreign investment decisions only to the extent that the host country meets other prerequisites for investment. It is the discretionary elements incorporated in the GSP schemes which prevent foreign investors from regarding duty-free access to export markets as a reliable and safe condition for medium-term investment.

Compared with the original objectives of the GSP, the schemes of the two major donors, as applied in practice, seem sadly deficient. Preferences schemes are regarded as a burden on the donor rather than as a path to trade liberalization which will help improve the internal allocation of resources. The restrictions embodied in the schemes severely limit the benefits which the GSP can bring to developing countries and, in many cases, render them nugatory.

GSP IN THE 1970s

There are not many (apart from politicians in developed countries) who would describe the GSP as undoubtedly successful. The few who consider it so might include the specialized discounters, wholesalers, mail-order houses, *et cetera*, which import low-priced finished goods from developing countries under intensive price competition. They are familiar with the mass of information concerning minutely defined origin rules, derogations from administrative procedures, time constraints for ordering and declaring goods, and so forth. Consumers in developed countries may benefit to some extent in terms of price competition and occasional special sales. Companies (or individuals) who have invested in developing countries and have set up organizations to export products on which preferential treatment has been restricted may also be satisfied with the schemes.

The donors have become aware, however, of wide differences among developing countries in taking advantage of the GSP. This has led to a gradual intensification of the discretionary and selective elements in their schemes, thus treating unequal trading partners within the developing countries unequally. The competitive-need rule in the American scheme or the ceiling limitations in the Community scheme for individual developing countries bear witness to this increasing complexity and restrictiveness. These rules implicitly introduced graduation long before it was explicitly implemented. Other restrictions stemmed from conflicting interests involving: (i) domestic suppliers in weak sectors, (ii) ministries of finance complaining about revenue losses, (iii) developing countries enjoying special preferences and, (iv) Community members over the allocation of the 'burden' and the limitations in the Community scheme.

The result of these developments soon became evident. The GSP was deprived of much of its potential effects on trade. In other words, preferences were eroded not so much because MFN tariff cuts reduced the margins of preference, but mainly because of administrative amputation. Preferences for successful exporters to the Community were frozen or, in the United States, denied, for products in which domestic suppliers had vested interests. Further, the smaller ,and poorer countries which were granted generous preferences could not take advantage of them probably because of their inability to compete in international markets for GSP products. The politics of good intentions is seldom good politics. This certainly applied during the 1970s to generalized preferences which were conceded under the influence of a misconceived mixture of fairness, tactics and selfishness.

Is the GSP Worthy of Reform?

Compared with issues such as non-tariff barriers, state trading, government procurement, export subsidies or 'evergreens' like protectionism in agriculture, the GSP has been a relatively minor issue in trade policy discussions between developed and developing countries. Is it nevertheless worth investing efforts to reform the GSP?

In order to answer this question, it is necessary to define the value of a properly functioning GSP. This value is much more than the preference margin times the import volume: it is first and foremost the guarantee of stable conditions for market access during the pay-off period of export-oriented investments. In this respect, long-term stability and simplicity of GSP conditions for individual export products is probably much more important than a large preference margin. Stability and simplicity would require the removal of the 'each product, each year' principle of conceding preferences. Moreover, safeguards with regard to special preferences (for example, those embodied in the Lomé Convention) should be phased out.

To overcome another major hurdle in the GSP schemes, the origin rules should be made much less restrictive. The value-added shares should be made cumulative for all developing countries and not for just the few which have formed customs unions. That is to say that if fabric, made in Korea or India, is imported into Hong Kong which then exports a finished garment to a developed country, then the value added in Korea or India as well as that in Hong Kong should be made the basis of the origin of the finished product. This could well have the effect of facilitating and encouraging the flow of capital and know-how from the advanced developing countries to the less advanced ones.

To summarize, though other issues may have more priority, there is a case for reforming the GSP. More transparency, stability, a longer time horizon and the removal of limitations which cause uncertainty and reluctance to invest should be the main yardsticks of reform. Discriminatory treatment between individual developing countries should be avoided as much as possible.

WHAT IS AT STAKE?

The direction in which the GSP is likely to evolve could well depend more on the implementation of the agreements reached in the Tokyo Round than on the annual technical modifications of the individual schemes. Two elements are of particular importance. One is the approval of special and differential treatment for the developing countries accompanied by the introduction of graduation. The other is the implementation of all the trade liberalizing measures agreed by the developed countries. The effectiveness of these measures in stimulating the exports of developing countries could, in turn determine whether MFN tariff cuts can regain some credit with the developing countries compared to the GSP.

Principle of Graduation

As far as the first element is concerned, the Agreement Relating to the Framework for the Conduct of International Trade which resulted from the Tokyo Round has important implications for the future of the GSP. After several years of negotiations, developing countries succeeded in obtaining legal rights for preferences in their favour. As a counterpart to granting special treatment to developing countries, however, the developed nations insisted on incorporating the principle of graduation into the new framework agreement. According to this principle, preferential treatment would be gradually withdrawn from individual advanced developing countries, depending on their development, and on their financial and trade needs. In addition, these countries would be expected to participate more fully in the GATT system of rights and obligations. Unfortunately, the agreement does not contain any guidelines for implementing the graduation principle.

The concept of graduation is clearly of significant importance, not only for the future of the GSP, but also for the entire range of international trade relations between developing and developed nations. As such it has generated an intense debate, both within and outside traditional international fora like GATT and UNCTAD. Several commentators in the developed countries have pointed out that some form of graduation is required in order to preserve an open international trading system. According to Isaiah Frank, indefinite and indiscriminatory preferential treatment for all developing countries would, in the long run, have adverse effects on both developing and developed countries.[1] In his view, 'by creating a permanent two-tier trading system, it would undermine ... efforts to strengthen international discipline over national trade policies and to foster the kind of open markets in which all countries, and especially those in the developing world, have a major stake'. Jere Behrman and T.N. Srinivasan take a similar stand based on the view that, because of their relative weakness, developing countries have the most to gain from a trading system of unconditional non-discrimination, predictability and transparency.[2]

Developing countries, however, generally oppose the principle of graduation, and they have concentrated their attacks on the way it has been implemented in practice. Most of all, they have criticized developed countries for introducing graduation measures unilaterally, thus contradicting the multilateral nature of the GSP. Developing countries demand, instead, that the introduction of graduation measures should be preceded by a multilateral agreement on the criteria to be used before they are implemented. Moreover, they insist that those criteria should be linked to a study of the implications of graduation in the context of the GSP for both graduated and graduating countries.[3]

A number of preference-giving countries have already adopted graduation policies, but so far only the Community and the United States have actually implemented them (see Chapter 2). They have done so in a discretionary manner, however, related more to their own internal pressure group interests than to objective criteria and this is undesirable.

The renewal of the American scheme enacted under the Trade and Tariff Act of 1984 provides for four types of graduation.[4] First, there is a new provisions on *country graduation*, under which the benefits of the scheme are to be terminated for any beneficiary whose GNP per capita income exceeds a certain dollar value adjusted annually ($US8,500 for 1984). Second, there is the *product graduation* mechanism provided by the competitive need limitations dating from the 1974 Trade Act. Third, is *discretionary product graduation*, applied since 1981, which was described in Chapter 5. Finally, there is a new provision for *accelerated product graduation*, which introduces more stringent competitive-need criteria for beneficiaries that have demonstrated 'a sufficient degree of competitiveness' in exporting particular GSP-eligible products.

At the same time, the 1984 Act authorizes the American President to waive the application of specific aspects of graduation in certain conditions. These conditions relate either to particular products or particular countries. Under this provision, a blanket waiver on the application of competitive-need limitations has been granted to the least developed countries. Other beneficiaries may also be granted a waiver regarding product graduation if the President determines that their actions on trade, investment, intellectual property and workers' rights are adequate.

Graduation will not change the fundamental problem of the competitive weakness of the poorer developing countries. It can, however, help to remove politically-rooted obstacles in developed countries against the penetration of products of special interest to these countries which compete strongly with domestic goods. For example, pressures by the Community for export restraint against a small supplier of knitwear, Mauritius (an ACP country), would probably not have been applied if the major exporters of knitwear from the Southeast Asian region had not received preferential treatment. In any event, if applied, graduation should be linked to objective criteria such as, though not exclusively, the level of *per capita* GNP.

Reduction of Tariffs

The second key element is the Tokyo Round of negotiated tariff cuts and their implementation in the 1980s. The developing countries take the view that these cuts will have a negative impact on their exports because of reductions in MFN duties which have already been made on products subject to GSP treatment. The erosion of GSP preference, however, is likely to be more than offset by gains from lower MFN tariffs on non-GSP products.[5] On the other hand, a major failure for developing countries has been the lack of agreement on a sensible system of safeguard conditions and procedures in cases of serious injury to competing domestic suppliers caused by imports. Safeguard conditions would have to be based on non-discrimination between all external suppliers.

The failure concerning non-discriminatory safeguard measures is of particular concern to the more advanced developing countries who increasingly face pressures to concede 'voluntary' export restraints and orderly marketing agreements. For these countries, non-discriminatory safeguard measures are more important than the GSP. Nevertheless, a properly functioning GSP could be of assistance to the export diversification efforts of the less advanced developing countries, provided that the GSP schemes are open-ended and include all sensitive as well as processed agricultural products.

A more promising route towards export diversification, however, might be:
  (a) the adjustment of distorted internal factor prices in developing countries through liberalization of their own import restrictions,
  (b) the elimination of distorting internal subsidies and
  (c) the adoption of realistic exchange rates.

If these changes took place, the export efforts of developing countries could be concentrated on those products in which they now have locational and comparative cost advantages. Greater potential for trade creation lies in this route and it would be preferable to a reliance on the possibility of trade diversion from developed countries, in response to preferential tariffs. Unfortunately, a really significant expansion of trade through these means can probably only be accomplished through multilaterally negotiated rather than unilaterally conceded tariff cuts. This is because political opposition would be likely if any one developing country unilaterally liberalized its trade as it would be felt that domestic interests were being threatened rather than third country interests in the developed world. Multilateral liberalization will be brought closer if efforts being made in the GATT to transform non-tariff barriers into tariff equivalents, which are negotiable, are successful. This could well be an important task for the projected new round of multilateral trade negotiations in the GATT.

THE FUTURE OF THE GSP

In essence, both the American and Community GSP schemes involve a 'rational protectionist's view of preference' aimed at controlling the amount and allocation of benefits among the beneficiaries.[6] Preferences for developing countries that are competitive in products for which the developed countries have a visible comparative disadvantage are often either not granted or withdrawn (competitive-need clause in the American scheme), or frozen (as in the Community scheme by means of rigid tariff quotas). On the other hand, preferences for developing countries which up to now have failed to convert a potential comparative advantage into a revealed comparative advantage, have been extended.

Both the GSP schemes reviewed in this essay reflect the overall tendency in international trade policy to discriminate against successful individual suppliers and to give in to domestic protectionist pressures, not only on a sectoral level but also on a product level. Such tendencies have seriously undermined both GSP schemes. Preferences in the GSP schemes are further reduced in value by MFN tariff cuts although these, in themselves, produce benefits for developing countries. At their present level, however, tariffs are probably no longer the most crucial barrier to entry for many products, and thus the GSP is no longer the most efficient way to eliminate export disincentives to developing countries.

In short, in the 1980s, the GSP is a minor aspect, and not the core of market access. Improvements in the schemes along the lines of more open-ended long-term guaranteed GSP conditions for individual products and beneficiaries will not change a great deal but, nevertheless, should be conceded. The focal point of reform, however, should be to encourage investment in developing countries by enterprises that are engaged in a world-wide intra-industry specialization. Such enterprises are at present restricted by the GSP origin rules in moving towards international specialization in the production process. Furthermore, investors need stability in GSP provisions during the pay-off period. This seems to be a much more important determinant of investment than a preferential zero tariff.

In the battle against protectionism, excessive effort should not be invested in the reform of the GSP. The major fight will be won or lost on the field of non-tariff barriers, and here the rapidly growing newly industrializing countries have a large contribution to make in offering reciprocity in the liberalization of their own markets.

NOTES AND REFERENCES

1. Isaiah Frank, *The 'Graduation' Issue in Trade Policy Toward LDCs*. World Bank Staff Working Paper No. 334 (Washington: 1979) and *Trade Policy Issues of Interest to the Third World*, Thames Essay No. 29 (London: Trade Policy Research Centre, 1981).

2. Jere R. Behrman, 'Rethinking Global Negotiations: Trade', in Jagdish Bhagwati and John G. Raggie (eds), *Power, Passions and Purpose: Prospects for North-South Negotiations*, (Cambridge: MIT Press,

1984) and T.N. Srinivasan, 'Why Developing Countries should Participate in the GATT System: The Third Harry G. Johnson Memorial Lecture', *The World Economy*, Vol. 5 (1982), pp. 85-104.

3. For further details on the position of developing countries, see UNCTAD, Report of the Special Committee on Preferences on its eleventh session. (Geneva, 1982).

4. This paragraph draws heavily on UNCTAD, *Ninth General Report on the Implementation of the Generalized System of Preferences*. Document TD/B/C.5/96, (Geneva: UNCTAD, 1985).

5. For confirmation of this point, see Sapir and Baldwin, 'India and the Tokyo Round', *World Development*, 11 July 1983, No. 7, pp. 565-74. This conclusion contradicts the findings made by UNCTAD, *Assessment of the Results of the Multilateral Trade Negotiations*, Document TD/B/778/Rev.1, (Geneva, 1982). The basic reason for these contrasting results lies in the methodologies which are used. For further discussion, see Sapir, *op. cit.*, and Baldwin and Murray, *op. cit.*

6. Johnson, *Economic Policies Toward Less Developed Countries*, *op. cit.*, pp. 199-201.

List of References

THIS list contains only the more important references cited in the text. The reader should refer to the Notes and References at the end of each chapter for more complete biographical information.

ROBERT E. BALDWIN and TRACY MURRAY, 'MFN Tariff Reductions and Developing Country Trade Benefits Under the GSP', *Economic Journal* 87, March 1977.

ROBERT E. BALDWIN, 'The Changing Nature of US Trade Policy since World War II', in Baldwin and Anne O. Krueger (eds), *The Structure and Evolution of Recent US Trade Policy* (Chicago: University of Chicago Press, 1984).

ROBERT E. BALDWIN, 'Trade Policies in Developed Countries', in Ronald W. Jones and Peter B. Kenen (eds), *Handbook of International Economics* (Amsterdam: North-Holland, 1984), Volume 1.

THOMAS BAYARD and M. MOORE, *Trade and Employment Effects of the US Generalized System of Preferences*, Office of Foreign Economic Research, US Department of Labor (Washington: 1979), mimeographed.

Jere R. Behrman, 'Rethinking Global Negotiations: Trade', in Jagdish Bhagwati and John G. Raggie (eds), *Power, Passion and Purpose*: Prospects for North-South Negotiations (Cambridge: MIT Press, 1984).

Axel Borrmann, Christine Borrmann, Manfred Steger, Das Allgemeine Zollpräferenzsystem der EG (Hamburg: Weltarchiv, 1979).

Kenneth Dam, *The GATT: Law and International Economic Organization* (Chicago and London: University of Chicago Press, 1970.

Isaiah Frank, *The 'Graduation' Issue in Trade Policy Toward LDCs*, World Bank Staff Working Paper No. 334 (Washington: 1979).

Isaiah Frank, *Trade Policy Issues of Interest to the Third World*, Thames Essay No. 29 (London: Trade Policy Research Centre, 1981).

Richard N. Gardner, *Sterling-Dollar Diplomacy* (Oxford: Clarendon Press, 1956).

Sidney Golt, *Developing Countries in the GATT System*, Thames Essay No. 13 (London: Trade Policy Research Centre, 1978).

Anwar Hoda, *GATT Reform and the Developing Countries*, Working Paper No. 7 (New Dehli: Indian Council for Research on International Economic Relations, 1983).

Robert Hudec, *Developing Countries in the GATT Legal System* (London: Trade Policy Research Centre, forthcoming).

Harry G. Johnson, *Economic Policies Toward Less Developed Countries* (Washington: Brookings Institution, 1967).

Karin Kock, *International Trade Policy and the GATT* (Stockholm: Almqvist and Wicksell, 1969).

Rolf J. Langhammer, *Ten Years of the EEC's Generalized System of Preferences for Developing Countries: Success or Failure?* Kiel Working Paper, No. 183, September 1983.

RACHEL McCULLOCH and JOSE PINERA, 'Trade as Aid: The Political Economy of Tariff Preferences for Developing Countries', *American Economic Review 67*, November 1977.

TRACY MURRAY, *Trade Preferences for Developing Countries* (New York: John Wiley, 1977).

RAUL PREBISCH, *Towards a New Trade Policy for Development* (New York: United Nations, 1964).

MICHAEL ROM, *The Role of Tariff Quotas in Commercial Policy* (London: Macmillan for the Trade Policy Research Centre, 1979).

ANDRÉ SAPIR and ROBERT E. BALDWIN, 'India and the Tokyo Round', *World Development*, 11 July 1983, No. 7.

T.N. SRINIVASAN, 'Why Developing Countries Should Participate in the GATT System: The Third Harry G. Johnson Memorial Lecture', The World Economy, Vol. 5 (1982).

ANN WESTON et al., *The EEC's Generalized System of Preferences* (London: Overseas Development Insitute, 1980).

ANN WESTON, 'Who is More Preferred? An Analysis of the New Generalized System of Preferences', in Christopher Stevens (ed.), *EEC and the Third World. A Survey. 2. Hunger in the World* (London: Overseas Development Institute and Institute for Development Studies, 1982).

MARTIN WOLF, 'Two-edged Sword: Demands of Developing Countries and the Trading System', in Jagdish Bhagwati and John G. Ruggie (eds), *Power, Passion and Purpose: Prospects for North-South Negotiations* (Cambridge, Mass: MIT Press, 1984).

Official Publications

A Guide to the U.S. Generalized System of Preferences (GSP), Office of the United States Trade Representative (Washington: 1983).

An Evaluation of US Imports under the Generalized System of Preferences, US ITC Publication 1379 (Washington: 1983).

EFTA, *The Trade Effects of EFTA and the EEC 1959-67* (Geneva: 1972).

OECD, *The Generalized System of Preferences: A Review of the First Decade* (Paris: OECD Secretariat, 1983).

Renewal of the Generalized System of Preferences, 98th Congress, 2nd session (Washington: Government Printing Office, 1984).

Report to the Congress on the First Five Years' operation of the United States Generalized System of Preferences (GSP), Committee on Ways and Means, US House of Representatives, 96th Congress, 2nd session (Washington: Government Printing Office, 1980).

Trends in International Trade. Report by a Panel of Experts (Geneva: GATT Sectretariat, 1958).

UNCTAD, *Assessment of the Results of the Multilateral Trade Negotiations*, Document TD/B/778/Rev.1 (Geneva, 1982).

UNCTAD, *Ninth General Report on the Implementation of the Generalized System of Preferences*, Document TD/B/C.5/96 (Geneva: UNCTAD, 1985).

UNCTAD, Report of the Special Committee on Preferences on its eleventh Session (Geneva: UNCTAD, 1985).

US Congress, *The Future of United States Foreign Trade Policy*, hearings before the Sub-committee on Foreign Economic Policy of the Joint Economic Committee, 90th Congress, 1st Session, Vol. 1 (Washington: Government Printing Office, 1967).

List of Thames Essays

OCCASIONAL papers of the Trade Policy Research Centre are published under the omnibus heading of Thames Essays. Set out below are the particulars of those published to date. The first 44 titles were published under the Centre's sole imprint, but they may also be obtained from the Gower Publishing Company, its address in the United Kingdom, the United States of America and Australia being set out in the reverse of the title page of this essay.

1 GERARD and VICTORIA CURZON, *Hidden Barriers to International Trade* (1970), 75 pp.

2 T.E. JOSLING, *Agriculture and Britain's Trade Policy Dilemma* (1970), 52 pp.

3 GERARD and VICTORIA CURZON, *Global Assault on Non-tariff Trade Barriers* (1972), 44 pp.

4 BRIAN HINDLEY, *Britain's Position on Non-tariff Protection* (1972), 60 pp.

5 GEOFFREY DENTON and SEAMUS O'CLEIREACAIN, *Subsidy Issues in International Commerce* (1972), 75 pp.

6 GEORGE F. RAY, *Western Europe and the Energy Crisis* (1975), 68 pp.

7 THEODORE GEIGER, JOHN VOLPE and ERNEST H. PREEG, *North American Integration and Economic Blocs* (1975), 65 pp.

8 HUGH CORBET, W.M. CORDEN, BRIAN HINDLEY, ROY BATCHELOR and PATRICK MINFORD, *On How to Cope with Britain's Trade Position* (1977), 80 pp.

9 PETER LLOYD, *Anti-dumping Actions and the GATT System* (1977), 59 pp.

10 T.E. JOSLING, *Agriculture in the Tokyo Round Negotiations* (1977), 48 pp.

11 HARALD B. MALMGREN, *International Order for Public Subsidies* (1977), 80 pp.

12 DAVID ROBERTSON, *Fail Safe Systems for Trade Liberalisation* (1977), 80 pp.

13 SIDNEY GOLT, *Developing Countries in the GATT System* (1978), 42 pp.

14 THEODORE HEIDHUES, T.E. JOSLING, CHRISTOPHER RITSON and STEFAN TANGERMANN, *Common Prices and Europe's Farm Policy* (1978), 83 pp.

15 HANS BÖHME, *Restraints on Competition in World Shipping* (1978), 92 pp.

16 ROBERT E. HUDEC, *Adjudication of International Trade Disputes* (1978), 95 pp.

17 STUART HARRIS, MARK SALMON and BEN SMITH, *Analysis of Commodity Markets for Policy Purposes* (1978), 91 pp.

18 ROBERT Z. ALIBER, *Stabilising World Monetary Arrangements* (1979), 51 pp.

19 ROBERT L. CARTER and GERARD M. DICKINSON, *Barriers to Trade in Insurance* (1979), *Out of Print*.

20 GEOFFREY SMITH, *Westminster Reform: Learning from Congress* (1979), 59 pp.

21 W.M. CORDEN, *The NIEO Proposals: a Cool Look* (1979). *Out of Print*.

22 ROBERT E. BALDWIN, *Beyond the Tokyo Round Negotiations* (1979), 46 pp.

23 DONALD B. KEESING and MARTIN WOLF, *Textile Quotas against Developing Countries* (1980), 226 pp.

24 M.FG. SCOTT, W.M. CORDEN and I.M.D. LITTLE, *The Case against General Import Restrictions* (1980), 107 pp.

25 VICTORIA CURZON PRICE, *Unemployment and Other Non-work Issues* (1980), 63 pp.

26 V.N. BALASUBRAMANYAM, *Multinational Enterprises and the Third World* (1980), 89 pp.

27 T.E. JOSLING, MARK LANGWORTHY and SCOTT PEARSON, *Options for Farm Policy in the European Community* (1981), 96 pp.

28 DEEPAK LAL, *Resurrection of the Pauper-labour Argument* (1981), 82 pp.

29 ISAIAH FRANK, *Trade Policy Issues of Interest to the Third World* (1981), 76 pp.

30 GEOFFREY SHEPHERD, *Textile-industry Adjustment in Developed Countries* (1981), 68 pp.

31 CHARLES COLLYNS, *Can Protection Cure Unemployment?* (1982), 95 pp.

32 BRIAN HINDLEY, *Economic Analysis and Insurance Policy in the Third World* (1982), 68 pp.

33 HUGH CORBET, *Beyond the Rhetoric of Commodity Power*, second edition (forthcoming).

34 BRIAN HINDLEY and ERI NICOLAIDES, *Taking the New Protectionism Seriously* (1983), 98 pp. Second edition forthcoming.

35 KENT JONES, *Impasse and Crisis in Steel Trade Policy* (1983), 108 pp.

36 CHARLES PEARSON, *Emergency Protection in the Footwear Industry* (1983), 101 pp.

37 MARTIN WOLF, HANS HINRICH GLISMANN, JOSEPH PELZMAN and DEAN SPINANGER, *Costs of Protecting Jobs in Textiles and Clothing* (1984), 163 pp.

38 JOSE DE LA TORRE, *Clothing-industry Adjustment in Developed Countries*, (1984), 286 pp.

39 KENNETH W. CLEMENTS and LARRY A. SJAASTAD, *How Protection Taxes Exporters* (1985), 87 pp.

40 T.G. CONGDON, *Economic Liberalism in the Cone of Latin America* (1985), 130 pp.

41 INGO WALTER, *Barriers to Trade in Banking and Financial Services* (1985), 136 pp.

42 BASIL S. YAMEY, RICHARD L. SANDOR and BRIAN HINDLEY, *How Commodity Futures Markets Work* (1985), 80 pp.

43 DAVID GREENAWAY and BRIAN HINDLEY, *What Britain Pays for Voluntary Export Restraints* (1985), 178 pp.

44 ELLIOT SCHRIER, ERNEST NADEL and BERTRAM RIFAS, *Outlook for the Liberalisation of Maritime Transport* (1986), 94 pp.

45 GARY BANKS and JAN TUMLIR, *Economic Policy and the Adjustment Problem* (1986), 101 pp.

46 RICHARD PRYKE, *Competition among International Airlines* (1987), 113 pp.

47 JAMES RIEDEL, *Myth and Reality of External Constraints on Development* (1987), 111 pp.

48 DAVID BEVAN, ARNE BIGSTEN, PAUL COLLIER AND JAN WILLEM GUNNING, *East African Lessons On Economic Liberalization* (1987), 72 pp.

49 ROLF J. LANGHAMMER AND ANDRÉ SAPIR, *Economic Impact of Generalized Tariff Preferences* (1987), 90 pp.

50 JIMMYE HILLMAN AND ROBERT ROTHENBERG, *Agricultural Trade and Protection in Japan*, forthcoming (1987).

51 DEEPAK LAL AND SARATH RAJAPATIRANA, *Impediments to Trade Liberalization in Sri Lanka*, forthcoming (1987).

52 ROMEO BAUTISTA, *Impediments to Trade Liberalisation in the Philippines*, forthcoming (1987).